QUANTUM
GRACE

This sequel completes a profoundly insightful Lenten companion for anyone yearning to connect the Incarnate Word, the contemporary revelations from the world of science, and the desire to "listen" to God's voice in our everyday lives. With a passion for prayer, a commitment to community, and a way with words, Judy Cannato has gifted the world with spiritual food for the journey. If you read only one book during the Lenten season, you will be well-fed if you read this one.

—Carol Zinn, SSJ
Congregations of St. Joseph

"Lent is a time to say yes in a new way," and in these reflections, are many invitations to new connections with the Holy mystery that sustains and nourishes us everyday.

—Diarmuid O'Murchu MSC

LENTEN REFLECTIONS
ON CREATION AND CONNECTEDNESS

QUANTUM
GRACE

THE SUNDAY READINGS

JUDY CANNATO

ave maria press AmP Notre Dame, Indiana

© 2005 by Ave Maria Press, Inc.

www.avemariapress.com

International Standard Book Number: 1-59471-024-4

Cover and text design by John Carson

Cover photo © Liquidlibrary

Printed and bound in the United States of America.

Library of Congress Cataloging-in-Publication Data

Cannato, Judy.
  Quantum grace : the Sunday readings / Judy Cannato.
    p. cm.
  ISBN 1-59471-024-4 (pbk.)
  1. Lent—Meditations. 2. Bible—Meditations. 3. Catholic Church.
Lectionary for Mass (U.S.). Sundays and feasts. I. Title.

  BX2170.L4C36 2005
  242'.34--dc22

                                    2004021048

For my mother,
Lucille Lemaster

CONTENTS

ACKNOWLEDGMENTS 9

INTRODUCTION 11

CYCLE A

First Sunday of Lent 19

Second Sunday of Lent 25

Third Sunday of Lent 29

Fourth Sunday of Lent 33

Fifth Sunday of Lent 37

Passion/Palm Sunday 41

CYCLE B

First Sunday of Lent 45

Second Sunday of Lent 51

Third Sunday of Lent 56

Fourth Sunday of Lent 61

Fifth Sunday of Lent 64

Passion/Palm Sunday 68

CYCLE C

First Sunday of Lent 73

Second Sunday of Lent 79

Third Sunday of Lent 85
Fourth Sunday of Lent 89
Fifth Sunday of Lent 93
Passion/Palm Sunday 97
Holy Thursday 101
Good Friday 105
Easter Vigil (Cycles A, B, C) 109
Easter Sunday (Cycles A, B, C) 115
Solemnities Celebrated in Lent
    March 19: St. Joseph, Husband of the
    Blessed Virgin Mary 119
    March 25: The Annunciation of the Lord 123

ACKNOWLEDGMENTS

My life continues to be filled with blessed connectedness and quantum grace, and I continue to be grateful for all those who are conduits of the Holy One's presence. All my relationships infuse my days with love, invite me to choose what is life-giving, and challenge me to abandon the temptation toward superficiality. I am grateful.

There are those to whom I want to express a special thanks:

Bob Hamma, editorial director at Ave Maria Press, for conversations and counsel that were invaluable; to Julia Hahnenberg and Karen Shannon for their editing skills.

Sallie Latkovich, CSJ, for reading the manuscript and for ongoing encouragement.

Jacquelyn Gusdane, SND, who continues to offer prayerful support and a listening heart.

The Sisters of St. Joseph of Cleveland, who offer the experience of community that invites me to grow.

Those whom I companion on the journey: your presence continues to be an inspiration and witness of quantum grace.

To my family—Phil, Philip, and Doug; my mother Lucille and Sister Linda; and Bill and Evelyn Cannato—who bless me with unreserved support and love.

And to the Holy One, the giver of quantum grace, the One who invites each of us to see the connectedness that is the foundation of all life.

INTRODUCTION

"Remember you are dust, and to dust you will return." With this reminder we are signed with ashes and begin the observance of Lent. We are dust, stardust, if we are to believe the insights of the new physics. Scientists tell us that all the matter that now exists was formed almost fourteen billion years ago and has been recycling ever since. We are part of a vast universe of energy particles that continues to renew and re-create. Literally, we are the dust of stars!

Prayer, fasting, and almsgiving are the disciplines traditionally associated with the season of Lent. We may pray more frequently, give up certain foods or habits, and make more effort to reach out to others in need. We usually make these efforts because we recognize that we have slipped away from living out our best intentions. We intuitively know that our relationships with God and one another are vital, yet we allow our attentiveness to diminish, caught up in the busy-ness of our lives. So once again we return to our Lenten observance, attending to the essential in our lives. This volume of *Quantum Grace* has been written as a companion to the first, continuing to look at Lent from a point of view that differs from the usual, and hopefully enabling us to see the scripture and the season in a new way, with fresh eyes that will renew us and free us to become more of who we truly are. The reflections are an attempt to break through our tendency to be superficial about matters we think are quite familiar.

The insights of the new physics are not only fascinating but tend to bring together scientific observation and religious belief in a way that alters how we perceive our world and how we relate to one another. If it is true that all the matter which now exists was formed so many billions of years ago, then the molecules that each of us calls "me" have already been part of someone or something else that has lived in the universe. And each of us will one day be part of someone or something else that has not yet existed. At the most fundamental level, we are all connected, and the notion that we are separate and set apart from others is illusion.

We experience our connectedness in many ways. As believers we have long known the ability of prayer to touch one another's lives in powerful ways, and now the new physics affirms that we don't have to be "on location" to influence the energy of someone or something else. Experiments have shown that once two photons bind, they are forever bound, whether the distance between them is a few centimeters or across the universe. In other words, once two energy fields connect—and each of us is an energy field—they are forever connected. We cannot *not* be connected. Should we be surprised, then, that a movement as slight as the ruffle of a butterfly's wing can change an energy pattern, as connected as we all are? And in a world described as a "global village," we can no longer avoid acknowledging that we are connected to all of life, that no one is really an alien or stranger.

The new physics tells us that on the subatomic level we can be described equally well as solid particles (like miniature billiard balls) or as waves (like undulations on the surface of the sea). In *The Quantum Self: Human Nature and Consciousness Defined by the New Physic*, contemporary physicist David Bohm says that "there is one energy that is the basis of all reality." His words resonate with what the mystics of religious traditions have been telling us all along, that we are one, all human beings, all creation. Unity—connectedness—is the foundation of life itself, and the energy that connects us flows from the Holy One, the divine creator who continues to form and fashion us, continues to ask us to remember who we are. And who are we? Cocreators, bidden by divine invitation to believe in incarnation.

The Incarnation we most readily recognize is that of Jesus, the one we call the Christ. Incarnation means "god in flesh," and as Christians we assent to the belief expressed in the hymn in the Second letter to the Philippians: "though he was in the form of God, [Christ] emptied himself, . . . coming in human likeness" and then "humbled himself, becoming obedient to death" (Phil 2:6–8). The Incarnation is that place of mystery where the human and divine intersect and are forever bound. In the intersection is where Jesus Christ stands, holding both divinity and humanity, restoring the connection that heals the rupture associated with Adam and Eve and fulfilling the covenant initiated by God.

If we suppose that the Incarnation is primarily about Jesus and only peripherally about us, however, we have limited its power and intention. Teresa of Avila speaks powerfully about our incarnation: "Christ has no body now but yours, no hands but yours, no feet but yours. Yours are the eyes through which he looks with compassion on this world." We are to continue to enflesh the mystery of the Incarnation in the concrete reality of our daily lives, and our observance of Lent can support us in the effort.

Although this volume of *Quantum Grace* focuses on the Sunday readings of Lent, the daily readings between Ash Wednesday and the first Sunday of Lent prepare us for what is to come throughout the season:

- "Choose life." (Thursday after Ash Wednesday) The words from Deuteronomy 30, spoken through Moses, convey God's command to the Israelites as they end their desert trek and are about to enter the Promised Land. They have been set free from slavery, and now they must learn to live in freedom. As all manner of things are set before them, life and death, blessings and curses, "Choose life" is the imperative given the chosen ones. The command is not an option, but a requirement for living in the land of promise. The scripture makes clear that the Israelites have the capacity to make life-giving choices—and of course, so do we. The commandments that are close by—in our mouths and on our hearts—are given to support us as we choose. Choosing life is closely associated with obedience, and authentic obedience does not impair our freedom but enhances it. The word obedience literally means "to listen" (*ob audire*), and choosing life requires the attentive listening that comes from the heart, that holy place where God longs to meet us.

- *"This, rather, is the fasting I wish."* (Friday after Ash Wednesday) A fast of giving up food or habits, symbolizing our desire to change, can be a significant gesture of self-denial, but unless our hearts really do change, the practice may be useless. The kind of fasting that God desires, Isaiah tells us, is this: releasing those bound unjustly, untying the thongs of the yoke, setting free the oppressed, sharing bread with the hungry, sheltering the oppressed and the homeless, clothing the naked when you see them, and not turning your back on your own (Is 58:6–7). This is a different kind of fasting, indeed. To attempt to do these things requires a self-denial that radically changes our perceptions and challenges us to facilitate what is life-giving for others. It is a fasting that focuses our attention not on ourselves and our failures but on our connectedness and our responsibility to choose life.

- *"Remove from your midst oppression."* (Saturday after Ash Wednesday) To do the kind of fasting God desires can

14

seem so overwhelming that we are tempted not to make the effort. There are so many who are unjustly bound, oppressed, hungry, homeless, and naked. How can we make a difference? The passage from Isaiah (58:9) does not excuse us from the demand, but makes the task a little more possible. If we attend to those *in our midst*—both by changing our attitudes and our actions—we can become part of an organic process of healing and reconciliation that will change the world. We begin by releasing those we have unjustly bound by our prejudices. We set free those we've enslaved with our expectations. We feed those who hunger for self-esteem and shelter those who reside in shame. We allow ourselves to stand naked and vulnerable before the Holy One, exposing the places where we need to be made whole. We clothe our relationships with truth and kindness of spirit.

We often tend to hold back and wait for others to get things started. During Lent God says, "Don't wait for others. Start right here, right now, in your midst. *You* choose life. *You* fast in a way that heals breaches. *You* remove oppression from your midst." This is what Jesus, the Incarnation, did. This is what his disciples are required to do as well. In this way the Incarnation continues and creationkind is restored to wholeness.

The German physicist Max Planck observed that energy does not travel in a straight line, but rather in waves or packets called "quanta." My experience of divine grace resonates with this image. I readily acknowledge that God's self-communication known as grace is always present, always available, yet there continue to be times in which the Holy One visits with waves or packets of exceptional clarity or inspiration, allowing me to see what I've missed or giving me the strength required to stay the course. These are times of "quantum grace." They seem to occur when I am most vulnerable, when my heart is rent and I have let go of my effort to control what is not mine to control. On Ash Wednesday we are asked to intentionally rend our hearts (Joel 2:13). We are then challenged to remain open for forty days, allowing God to enter and perhaps impart a measure of quantum grace.

Observing Lent through the lens of the new physics can help us see freshly. How does recognizing that our energy is connected to others—and that we don't have to be "on location" to influence another person's energy—change the way we pray? How does knowing that two energy fields, once connected, are forever bound together change the way I think about relationships, old and new? How does "connectedness" impact the kind of fasting that has to do with releasing the unjustly bound and setting free the oppressed? We know that whatsoever we do to the least of our sisters and brothers we do to Christ. The new physics resonates with this truth, asserting that what we do to or for others we do to or for ourselves. As members of the body of Christ, we are all connected, our lives intertwined in love or fear, depending upon which we choose.

Knowing that the ruffle of a butterfly's wings can change the flow of energy, what does that imply about almsgiving? Our effort, our energy, so much greater than that of a delicate butterfly wing, *does* have power to influence and create change. The new physics affirms the experience of the old mystics. We are one—all of us, all creation. The new physics together with the tenets of our faith help us respond in a fresh, imaginative way to the question, "Who are we?" *Quantum Grace* suggests this response: We are human beings created by the Holy One and invited to take our place as cocreators who will restore and renew the face of the universe. Lent is a time to say yes in a new way—yes to being who we are intended to be.

How to Use This Book

This volume of *Quantum Grace* contains reflections on the Sunday readings of Lent for Cycles A, B, and C, Holy Thursday, Good Friday, the Easter Vigil, and Easter Sunday. In addition, St. Joseph's Day and the Annunciation, solemnities that normally fall within the season of Lent, are also included. Each entry lists the scripture readings of the day, then offers a reflection that comes through a framework inspired by the new physics. The entry concludes with suggestions for further reflection and journaling. Most days have several questions, so you may want to choose the one that draws the most attention or the most resistance. The questions conclude with the invitation to pray, to take your own insights to the Holy One who is eager for connection.

May this Lenten season be one in which you are filled with quantum grace. May you rediscover the connectedness that is at the heart of all of life, and may the love of the Holy One call you deeply into the awareness of who you are—a cocreator—with the capacity to choose life, not only for yourself, but for creationkind.

First Sunday of Lent

(Cycle A)

Scripture Readings:
Genesis 2:7–9; 3:1–7
Psalm 51
Romans 5:12–19
Matthew 4:1–11

One does not live by bread alone. . . .

The readings from this first Sunday of Lent remind us what the Lenten season is about. Just four days ago we were signed with ashes, remembering we are dust—stardust. The daily scriptures for the remainder of the week have been full of sound instruction that will help us proceed through this season faithfully. On Ash Wednesday we were asked to rend our hearts, to tear them wide open and expose them to the Holy One who longs to point out the places that need to be changed and the places that need to be healed. Thursday's readings brought us the commandment "choose life," which implies listening and obeying.

The scriptures from Friday remind us that the kind of fasting that God wants is this: to release those unjustly bound, to untie the thongs of the yoked, to set free the oppressed, share bread with the hungry, shelter the homeless, clothe the naked, and not turn our backs on our own. To keep us from being overwhelmed by such daunting tasks, Saturday's reading from Isaiah gives us help: remove *from your midst* oppression, false accusation, and malicious speech. As we tend to those in our midst, we enter into an organic process that brings healing and wholeness to all creation.

On this first Sunday of Lent we hear two tales of temptation. The first is the story of the ancestors we call Adam and Eve. It is not easy to hear the story of "the fall" clearly, for we often bring to it false assumptions and inaccurate details. In this passage from Genesis, Adam and Eve have not yet been named. They are simply referred to as "the man" and "the woman," words that literally mean "dust from the ground" or "groundlings." The serpent, created by God to be particularly crafty and cunning, is not labeled as evil. In this narrative the serpent is simply a functional character used to introduce doubt into the mind of the woman, whose daily life until now has involved walking in the garden with God.

The serpent begins by distorting the command Yahweh has given the man and woman. "Did God really tell you not to eat from any of the trees in the garden?" The woman sets the serpent straight: "We may eat of the fruit of the trees in the garden; it is only about the fruit of the tree in the middle of the garden that God said, 'You shall not eat it or even touch it, lest you die.'" The tree under discussion is the tree of the knowledge of good and evil. The serpent gives a cunning reply: "God knows well that the moment you eat of it your eyes will be opened and you will be like gods who know what is good and what is bad." The comment gives the woman pause—and this is the moment that is significant, for it is the first time in scripture we see a human being engaging the freedom to choose. Already something has happened. Something within human consciousness has altered, and human life will never be the same again.

As the woman looks at the tree, she sees that it is good for food, that it is pleasing to the eye and desirable for obtaining wisdom. None of these observations is inaccurate. The scripture does not say that she wants to be like God. There appears to be no malevolence on her part, for evil has not yet entered the human picture. The woman simply chooses not to obey God. She takes the fruit, eats, and shares it with the man. It is then that they recognize they are naked and cover themselves with fig leaves.

We know that the word "obedience" comes from *ob audire*, which means "to listen." The woman has chosen not to listen. She has ears to hear but does not hear. She is not yet aware of the gifts that she does possess. The woman already has the capacity for recognizing what is good; she already appreciates the beautiful; she already desires wisdom—all very good things that flow out of her connectedness with the Creator. But as a result of her refusal to act on what she has heard, she will now know evil and will be required to identify and reject it. This action moves her into a new consciousness, and with the move the ease of living in intimate connectedness with Yahweh, with the man, and even with herself will be gone.

It is after this experience that the woman is given the name Eve, "mother of all the living." Indeed, we are her offspring, for we know well the temptation to doubt or meddle with what we have heard and to act without attention or awareness. We know the desire to move ahead of grace and the tendency to blame others for our falls. We know the pain of ruptured connections, even as we remember the peaceful moments of walking with the Holy One. We share the blindness she experiences—having eyes, but not seeing the power that accompanies the ability to choose.

There is no such blindness in Jesus. He does not fall prey to the tactics of the tempter, for he sees precisely what Satan is up to. Jesus is aware of his power to choose, and he exercises that power to refute every temptation. He will not use his power to turn any kind of stone into any kind of bread. As famished as he must be, his hunger for the things of God remains greater than his hunger for food. The reply that enables Jesus to refute his adversary is important for us to hear as well: "One does not live by bread alone, but by every word that comes forth from the mouth of God." Unlike Eve, Jesus does not reject the word of God. He does not confuse what he is about with what God is about. He is obedient—able to listen and respond to the Holy One in a way that does not make too much or too little of his own power.

We can allow these two temptation narratives to question us: Where do we lack awareness because we have failed to be attentive? How do we deal with our power? Eve is unable to recognize how truly empowered she is. Jesus recognizes his empowerment without abusing or misusing it. He knows what is his to do, and he knows what is God's to do. He is cocreative in his response, open and availing himself to God's grace.

At the beginning of this season that invites us to become more attentive and aware, let us feed on the words that come from the Holy One's mouth and let them expose and heal our hearts. Let us invite God to point out the blind places within us. Let us ask God to help us become aware of the power we have, and to show us where we use it well and where we do not, where we have given our power over to others out of fear, and where we have used our power to choose life.

For Reflection/Journaling:

- I become aware of a time when I was tempted and failed to use my power well. I am attentive to the thoughts and feelings that surface.
- I recall a time when I was tempted and used my power to choose life. I am attentive to the thoughts and feelings that surface.
- I bring my reflection to prayer. . . .

Second Sunday of Lent

(Cycle A)

Scripture Readings:
  Genesis 12:1–4a
  Psalm 33
  2 Timothy 1:8b–10
  Matthew 17:1–9

This is my beloved . . . listen to him.

Abram hears God's call to leave the land of his kinsfolk and to move to an undisclosed location. The call is a summons that holds the promise of relationship and blessing for Abram and Sarai, their family, and their descendants. The passage notes Abram's seventy-five years of age, as if to say that he is old enough to be wise. There is no report that Abram objects or asks for more details. We are told simply, "Abram went."

The reading from Second Timothy says that we are called to a holy life, and that holiness is not determined by how much we do but by how much grace we receive. The "work" has already been done and is manifested through Christ Jesus. We have only to receive the grace that continues to pour forth from God's hand. In the reading from Leviticus earlier in the week (Monday), God reminds the Israelites to "be holy, for I, the Lord, your God, am holy" (19:2). Holiness for a people who has experienced exile is about keeping themselves separate in order to preserve their culture and identity. Jesus, as we know, reverses this notion of holiness, making it more about inclusion than exclusion, and this upsets those who hold religious power and use it for their own purposes. Being holy in this way brings hardship for Jesus, and, according to Timothy's letter, it will bring hardship for us, if we decide to live this way.

Being holy, as Jesus demonstrates, is about living out of the connectedness that is our fundamental reality. We cannot choose *not* to be connected; we can only attend to the quality of the connections in our lives. There is an old story that asks the question, How do you know if a certain person is really holy? The response that comes back is: "Because I feel holy when I am with them." Genuine holiness opens us up. Genuine holiness connects us heart-to-heart. Genuine holiness pulls us into the awareness of who we are—cocreators with the Holy One, responsible for choosing life and empowering one another. We know, both from the gospel and from our own experience, that Jesus' kind of holiness, the holiness of inclusion, is not well received by everyone, least of all from those who profit from remaining separate and apart. They prefer to remain in the illusion that has allowed them to be comfortable. Without recognizing that they are rooted in fear, they hold their ground and will not permit their hearts to be coaxed open.

In the account of the Transfiguration we are reminded that Jesus, like Abram, has been invited into a new land. The land of promise for Jesus—and for all who choose to follow—will be known as the reign of God. Peter and James and John are privileged not only to witness this significant event, but to have integral roles in the unfolding of the dream. As they are present with Jesus on the mountaintop, God speaks to them: "This is my beloved Son, with whom I am well pleased; listen to him." We hear that word again— "listen"—which implies obedience. This is an important revelation for Peter, James, and John, for they have witnessed Jesus' faithful, obedient listening to the Holy One. Now God discloses that listening to Jesus is the same as listening to the divine. God makes known to these disciples who Jesus is— which in turn tells them who they are. This is a moment of transfiguration for them as well.

The appearance of Moses and Elijah strengthens Jesus in this critical moment of his life. These are the perfect companions and counselors for Jesus as he strives to listen obediently and use his power in the service of love. It was Moses who time and again interceded for the Israelites, who stood in the gap between them and God, mediating healing. It was Moses who received the law that would enable the chosen ones to fulfill their part of the covenant. It was Elijah, with the name that means "Yahweh is my God," who learned to hear God in a whisper and who discerned the false from the true. It was Elijah who burned like fire in his passion for God.

In this vision on the mountaintop these two prophets attend to Jesus, preparing him for the "hardship for the gospel" that will mean his suffering and death. Like Moses, he will stand in the breach between the human and the divine and mediate healing. He will remain firm in fidelity to the law—the truth of the law, not some distorted version of it. Like Elijah, his whole life cries out "Yahweh is my God!" Falsehood will not only be exposed, but consumed by the passionate fire of love. Here, in this moment on the mountaintop, Jesus receives what he needs to continue his mission. It is a moment of quantum grace for Jesus. Listen to him.

For Reflection/Journaling:

- I bring to mind a person who allows me to experience my own holiness. What is it about this person that stirs my heart and calls me to deeper connectedness? I search for that quality within myself and affirm it. I ask for a blessing on the person who allows me to experience my holiness.
- Who are the prophets in my life—those who help me listen to the voice of the Holy One? I recall a message that has been difficult to hear and explore the lessons I have learned from the experience.
- I bring my reflection to prayer. . . .

Third Sunday of Lent

(Cycle A)

Scripture Readings:
Exodus 17:3–7
Psalm 95
Romans 5:1–2, 5–8
John 4:5–42

Whoever drinks the water I shall give will never thirst.

We can live a month without food. We can live only a week without water. In a desert culture like the one known to the Israelites, water was in short supply, and to have no water meant that death would come very soon. It is not surprising, then, that the life of a community revolved around the water source.

Today's readings are filled with images of water and thirst. From within the experience of a desert land, we hear the cry of the psalmist:

O God, you are my God whom I seek;
for you my flesh pines and my soul thirsts
like the earth, parched, lifeless and without
water. (Ps 63:2)

This thirst is a longing that is soul deep, a pining from a place where life meets death and seeks at least a sip, so that death will disappear.

It is thirst for water that sets the Israelites to grumbling against Moses. Dehydrated and unable to think clearly, they ask him, "Why did you ever make us leave Egypt?" In their physical thirst they have become disconnected from the memory of who they are and what God has done for them. Do they really prefer slavery? No. They are simply afraid of death, and at this moment surviving in slavery seems preferable to dying in the parched, apparently lifeless desert. Moses himself is afraid that these people in his charge will rise up and stone him. They equate water with God's presence, asking, "Is the Lord in our midst or not?"

The image of water predominates the gospel as well. The setting is near the town of Sychar, in Samaria, at Jacob's well. We recall that Jacob, like the Israelites who trekked through the desert, was a survivor. And so is the woman Jesus meets there, as we learn more about her. Jews considered Samaritans to be unclean, but even the unclean thirst. And thirst is what Jesus uses to lure the woman into an experience of connectedness that will change her life—and the life of her town. The encounter begins with a simple request: "Give me a drink." Of course the woman is surprised. "How can you, a Jew, ask me, a Samaritan woman, for a drink?" Jesus has just broken two carefully observed boundaries: he, a man, has spoken to her, a woman, in public; he, a Jew, has spoken to her, a Samaritan. In addition, with a bucket that is considered unclean, to drink from it would violate another boundary.

We know from the account of Jesus' temptation in the desert that he will not turn stone into bread, no matter how hungry he is. Here he will once again defer satisfying his own physical need in order to quench the parched soul of another human being. His food and drink, we know, come from the mouth of God. Even though physical thirst is the language used, it is the deeper thirst—the heart's longing for the Holy One—that holds the real meaning of the encounter.

Jesus tells the woman that if she knew who he really is, she would ask him for a drink and receive "living water." Continuing to speak in physical terms, the woman asks him where this water is. She seems to refer to running water, wanting access to a more convenient source. Jesus clarifies: "Everyone who drinks this water will be thirsty again; but whoever drinks the water I shall give will never thirst." The water will be an inner well, a fountain that never dries up. Like the thirsty Israelites who grumble to Moses, Jesus equates the presence of water with the presence of God.

The woman is attracted to the convenience. She wants this living water so that she will not be physically thirsty and will no longer be burdened with coming to this well in the heat of noon-day. But Jesus will no longer allow her to escape the real issue at hand. "Go call your husband and come back." She answers with a half-truth: "I do not have a husband." Jesus' response indicates that he has a deeper knowledge of her than she has revealed to him. "You have had five husbands, and the one you have now is not your husband." He does not judge her half-truth, but affirms, "What you have said is true." She declares that he is a prophet and tries to maneuver the discussion away from her personal life and into a larger arena. She wants to talk about the beliefs that have divided her people and his, people who once shared the connectedness of being the chosen ones.

But this prophet is not interested in the broader religious picture at the moment. He is interested in *her* life, her belief. He dismisses the question altogether, because the hour has come when worshiping in spirit and truth is more significant than worshiping in any particular geographical location. When the woman mentions the coming of the Christ, who "will tell us everything," Jesus reveals to her "I am he." Her response is to leave her water jar behind and run to the town, where she tells the people, "Come see a man who told me everything I have done. Could he possibly be the Messiah?"

The living water begins to renew her and the other thirsty Samaritans of the town. Because of the woman's testimony, they invite Jesus to remain with them. He stays two days, but the water surely remains long after. With their parched hearts now filled with the presence of God, they declare, "we know that this is truly the savior of the world." The water of life brings them to the presence of God, and they will never be thirsty again.

For Reflection/Journaling:

- I imagine myself in a desert climate, my throat parched. I long for water.
- I thirst most for. . . .
- I drink a glass of water slowly, reflectively. I imagine the water seeping into every cell of my body, quenching not only my physical thirst, but the thirst of my spirit.
- I bring my reflection to prayer. . . .

Fourth Sunday of Lent

(Cycle A)

Scripture Readings:
1 Samuel 16:1b, 6–7, 10–13a
Psalm 23
Ephesians 5:8–14
John 9:1–41

I was blind and now I see.

The weekday readings have prepared us for this fourth Sunday of Lent. Through the story of Naaman the leper we are reminded that our God is a God who heals. The account of Shadrach, Meshach, and Abednego is about fidelity—human and divine. The unthankful servant helps us remember the value of gratitude, while the words of Moses stress the importance of remembering what our own eyes have seen. In the gospel accounts we see the growing tension between Jesus and the Pharisees, how his words divide the true from the false, the righteous from the unrighteous.

Finally, we hear the great commandment, to love the Holy One with our whole heart and soul and mind and strength, the proper response to the God who asks for only one thing: "It is love that I desire."

Today's readings are filled with images of connectedness and disconnectedness.

The passage from First Samuel depicts the anointing of David. As the oil is poured over David's head, the spirit of God rushes upon him, and his life will depend upon maintaining a connectedness with God in behalf of his people. David provides a historical connection to Jesus, his descendent who is also anointed with the spirit in order to serve his people. The psalmist sings,

> You spread the table before me
>> in the sight of my foes;
>> you anoint my head with oil;
>> my cup overflows. (Ps 23:5)

Anointing, we are reminded, is not without controversy, and while Jesus overflows with the spirit, his foes are everywhere.

The theme of darkness and light is taken up in the reading from the epistle to the Ephesians. We are reminded that we were once in darkness and have been brought into the light by Christ. We are to take no part in the fruitless works of darkness but remain assured by the promise that "Christ will give you light." It is the light of Christ which is the sign that we live in vital connection to the Holy One.

The conflict between darkness and light is brought to the fore in the gospel narrative of the man born blind. Jesus is dealing with blindness of two kinds. In the first case, a young man who has been blind since birth is brought to Jesus to be healed. The disciples—sincere in their attempt to live in the light—ask Jesus the cause of the man's blindness, with its side effects of social and religious disconnection. Was it his sin or the sin of his parents that has caused the blindness? In their worldview, disease and physical disability were seen as consequences of sin. Jesus rejects such a notion.

The second kind of blindness involves the neighbors who question the healing and the Pharisees who question the one healed. The neighbors debate whether this really is the man who used to sit at the gate and beg. Some think it is, while others are of the opinion that "he just looks like him." When they ask the young man, "How were your eyes opened?" he tells them the whole story: "The man called Jesus made clay and anointed my eyes and told me, 'Go to Siloam and wash.' So I went there and washed and was able to see." He tells it simply, but complications set in.

Brought before the Pharisees, the healed man is questioned once again. There is great controversy because Jesus has broken the law by healing on the sabbath. There is no hint of joy or celebration over what has happened in their midst—that the blind now sees—just indignation that Jesus has broken the law. In the Pharisees' dialogue with the young man, their own blindness becomes more visible. It is evident that these religious leaders live in a small, dark world, narrow in its interpretation of the law and darkened by its connection to fear, suffocating the spirit that continually calls them into the light. These are the truly blind, for they can no longer see the truth that is in front of them. They are incapable of recognizing that the fulfillment of the law they so protectively guard is right before their eyes. The healing of the young man's physical blindness exposes the spiritual blindness of the Pharisees, a blindness that cannot envision the true and the good. Sadly, their blindness cannot be healed, simply because they will not admit that they cannot see.

The light of Christ brings vision—and division. The light of Christ, when we yield to it, exposes the blindness that we all have. For all of us, individually and collectively, there are places in our lives where we cannot see. Our connectedness to the light may be ruptured and we may find ourselves sitting in the darkness of fear. Just as there is no sin in the young man's being born blind, there is no sin in our having blind spots. But living unaware and inattentive to blind spots can cause us to miss the mark. The light of Christ, when we allow it to permeate the eyes of our hearts, can reveal the illusions and the prejudices that disable us and the fear-filled narrow places that suffocate the spirit. Perhaps the process of healing of our hearts will not happen as quickly as the healing of the blind man's eyes, but our healing will come as we become ever more open to the radiance of Christ's love. The healing of sight is promised to all who are willing to acknowledge the truth: that we are all blind in some way and that without the light of Christ none of us can see.

For Reflection/Journaling:

- I ask God to expose the places in me that suffer from blindness. (It is often possible to become aware of blind spots when we scan our memory for a time that was stressful and/or involved significant interaction with others and called for decision-making.) As I name these vulnerable places within me, I hold them gently in the light of Christ's love.
- Without judgment, I examine blindness that I see around me, in my midst, in the world. I hold each blindness in the light of Christ's love.
- I place myself in the gospel story and enter into conversation with the young man born blind.
- I bring my reflection to prayer. . . .

Fifth Sunday of Lent

(Cycle A)

Scripture Readings:
    Ezekiel 37:12–14
    Psalm 130
    Romans 8:8–11
    John 11:1–45

Do you believe?

"You shall know that I am the Lord, when I open your graves and have you rise from them, O my people!" These are the words God speaks to the Israelites through the prophet Ezekiel. Since only God can bring the dead back to life, any rising from the grave will be a sign that the Holy One is present.

We have seen throughout the Lenten season how persistent our God is. Invitation after invitation, the Holy One seeks to be known. Time after time the voice of God proclaims with great passion a love that refuses to die. Day after day the Holy One waits, restrained only by respect for human freedom, hoping today will be the day that humankind returns to love. During the weekday readings we have heard God's desire to create new heavens and a new earth, and we have seen signs of new life as Jesus heals the sick and seeks to teach his people how to connect to God in love.

Tension has been building as Jesus' reputation grows. There are those who choose to believe in love, while others stay rooted in the kind of fear and egocentricity that expresses itself in wickedness. The conspiracy that will result in Jesus' death begins to swell, and no bystander seems to escape the questions suspended in the air: Do you believe in the possibility of Paradise? Do you believe new heavens and a new earth are not only possible, but have come? Do you believe that God has truly visited us in the flesh? There appear to be no blurred lines, only the clear-cut question and a required response: yes or no.

Today's reading from Romans is one we need to be clear about. Paul says, "Those who are in the flesh cannot please God." Too often rejection of our human nature has resulted from thinking that somehow the human body or human person is in essence depraved. We are embodied spirits, and current theology and related disciplines affirm the holistic nature of the human person. What Paul seems to understand is that within each of us there is a battle going on, a battle between two contrary tendencies, each of which wants to have its way with us. One, the "flesh," is what today we may call egocentricity and self-absorption, while the other is the spirit that seeks to live in unity and love. We are meant to live *pneuma*-centric, not egocentric, lives.

Jesus is the Word made flesh—and so to think that his fleshly nature was not human pushes us onto shaky theological ground, for a fundamental tenet of our faith asserts that Jesus was *fully* human. In Jesus, the Word became wholly human and entered into that place of conflict where egocentricity and self-absorption struggle against the spirit of the Holy One within us. And through Jesus—the definitive expression of quantum grace—we have new life in the spirit, as ones who have been brought back from the grave. The gospel story of Lazarus, then, becomes the story of each of us. Lazarus is Jesus' friend, and apparently Jesus frequents his home in Bethany, where Lazarus lives with his sisters Martha and Mary. Jesus loves them, and it seems that these friends experience an unusual kind of connectedness in the relationships they share.

There is danger for Jesus as he returns to Bethany, for the conspiracy against him is gaining momentum. Jesus is a man with a price on his head, and his return to the area of Jerusalem places him at risk. Because of his love he responds to the sisters' request, but along the way Jesus informs his disciples that Lazarus is already dead.

It is Martha who comes out to meet Jesus as he approaches their home. Never afraid to speak her mind, she says to her friend, "If you had been here, my brother would not have died." She knows Jesus. She has undoubtedly witnessed him touch and heal the deaf and the blind and the lame. She has experienced in his presence the power of God. She had wanted to see that healing and power cure her brother. "Your brother will rise," Jesus tells her. She finds no comfort in his words. Still dissatisfied, she says to Jesus, "I know he will rise, in the resurrection on the last day." She does not know the healing and power she is about to witness, nor the revelation her friend is about to speak.

"I am the resurrection and the life," Jesus announces to Martha, "whoever believes in me, even if he dies, will live, and everyone who lives and believes in me will never die." The question he asks Martha is for us, too: "Do you believe this?" His friend and disciple replies, "Yes, Lord. I have come to believe that you are the Messiah, the Son of God, the one who is coming into the world." Aware of who stands with her, Martha still grieves for the brother who is dead.

Mary then comes out to Jesus, and she repeats what her sister has said, "If you had been here, my brother would not have died." She, too, believes that in Jesus' presence there is life and in his absence there is death. Together they weep over the death of Lazarus. And then Jesus asks, "Where have you laid him?"

Those who have been comforting the sisters have followed Mary out to meet Jesus, and they begin to murmur, "Could not the one who opened the eyes of the blind man have done something so that this man would not have died?" Jesus is perturbed by their remarks but continues to the place where Lazarus is buried. When he asks some of the mourners to roll the stone away from the entrance to the tomb, Martha protests, knowing that Lazarus has been dead for four days and there will be a stench.

It is then that Jesus prays, not for himself, but for the crowd, "that they may believe that you sent me." Ezekiel's long-awaited prophecy is about to be fulfilled. Jesus cries out in a loud voice, "Lazarus, come out!" And Lazarus appears. Wrapped in burial cloths, Lazarus comes out. The grave has opened up and he who was dead arises. Surely God is present!

For Reflection/Journaling:

- I recall a time when I felt lifeless. I consider how God's grace was present in my rising back to life.
- I look to see if there are any lifeless places within me now, and ask the Holy One to touch that place. What do I need to do to participate in the "unbinding"?
- I write a profession of faith, a statement of what I believe.
- I bring my reflection to prayer. . . .

Passion/Palm Sunday

(Cycle A)

Scripture Readings:
Matthew 21:1–11 (The Procession with Palms)
Isaiah 50:4–7
Psalm 22
Philippians 2:6–11
Matthew 26:14–27:66

Who is this?

Jesus enters into Jerusalem riding a colt, surrounded by believers and the curious—a very large crowd crying out, "Hosanna to the Son of David!" The road is covered with cloaks from their backs and branches from their trees. The whole city is shaken and asks, "Who is this?" The question is the one we carry as we enter the observance with our own palm branches.

There has been a progression to the readings we have experienced during these Sundays of Lent. We recall that on the first Sunday there were two temptation stories—one involving the woman and man we call Eve and Adam, the other involving Jesus. Both stories affirm the gift of human freedom and point to our need to make choices that are cocreative and life-giving. The readings for the second Sunday examine the call to live a holy life. Jesus, connected to the Holy One in a definitive way, shows us by example that holiness is about inclusion rather than exclusion and must flow out of the impulse to love rather than the impulse to control. The next three Sundays show us the kinds of choices we must make in order to be holy. We must choose between living in thirst or living satiated by the water of life. We must decide whether to walk in darkness or in light, blind or sighted. We must choose between death and life. Living in holiness will mean living with thirst quenched, vision restored, and life full—but these gifts will not come without great openness and vulnerability, effort and grace, and the death of many illusions.

Now, on this day we call Passion Sunday, we are drawn into the drama of Jesus' final hours and asked to respond to the question ourselves, "Who is this?" Who is this man Jesus, and what is the meaning of his life for our lives? Our response matters, not because it decides anything about who Jesus is, but because it decides everything about who we are.

The Jesus in Matthew's gospel is one who is fully aware of what is going on around him, fully aware of the cup he is about to drink. The gospel reading begins with Jesus' statement, "One of you will betray me." Indeed, the connections that have been vital to Jesus are being tested, and most will appear to rupture and disengage under the strain. Before the Passover meal is shared, Judas has already collected his thirty pieces of silver. Peter boldly professes to Jesus, "Even though I should have to die with you, I will not deny you." He is not alone in his illusion, for "all the disciples spoke likewise." Within a short time they will have scattered, watching the proceedings from a distance, renouncing their connection to the one who continues to call each of them "friend."

Throughout his ministry Jesus has endeavored to connect with the religious authorities who prefer to live under the illusion that they are separate and apart. Challenging them to notice their blindness, he extends the possibility of vision and light. Challenging them to notice their thirst for the Holy One, he extends the cup of living water. But they want no part of the kind of connection Jesus represents, and instead conspire to have him crucified. They turn him over to Pilate, who washes his hands of the matter, unable to connect to the truth that stands before him.

There have been so many who have reached out to Jesus, listening to his words, asking to follow or be healed. Now, as one by one they withdraw, Jesus appears more and more alone. The crowds that cried "Hosanna" have broken away and now call out, "Crucify him!" As he hangs on the Cross he is reviled by those who taunt, "Save yourself" and, "Come down from the cross." Even the revolutionaries who are hanging on crosses at either side abuse him. When he cries out, *"Eli, Eli, lema sabachthani?"* all connectedness appears to be broken, for even God seems to have turned away.

There is nothing to suggest that Jesus felt anything but disconnection as he hung on the Cross—cut off from disciples and friends, religious and political authorities, those he had touched and healed, even the Holy One. At times we profess that Jesus "descended into Hell" on our behalf in that time and space between his death and resurrection. Perhaps this moment on the Cross is that Hell—the experience of having no sense of connection with anyone anywhere.

Yet Jesus refuses to become disconnected. His cry, "My God, my God, why have you forsaken me?" is itself a declaration of connection. *My* God—Jesus continues to claim the relationship from which he takes his identity. This is the definitive moment, the moment when Jesus completes his mission—by remaining connected regardless of his feelings, regardless of appearances, regardless of rejection and pain and suffering and death. This is the greatest moment of quantum grace, the moment that the representative of the humanity that first bought into the illusion of separateness refuses to allow anything to get in the way of being faithful to the truth of connectedness. This experience heals the connection that God longs to have healed. This is the return with a whole heart, and through it we are all saved, no longer under the spell of the illusion that we are disconnected from one another and from God, but exposed once again to the truth that has been there all along: we are one, all of us, we are one. Today we are called to look at this moment on the Cross, to ask, "Who is this?" and then to plumb the depths of our hearts for a response. The question hangs on the Cross and will not go unanswered.

For Reflection/Journaling:

- I sit quietly and allow the gospel scene to unfold in my imagination. As I immerse myself in the Passion, I ponder the question, "Who is this?" and put into words or an image my response.
- I examine my life for places that seem disconnected and bring them to this moment of transformation at the Cross.
- I bring my reflection to prayer. . . .

First Sunday of Lent

(Cycle B)

Scripture Readings:
Genesis 9:8–15
Psalm 25
1 Peter 3:18–22
Mark 1:12–15

Recall the covenant I have made. . . .

Let us be reminded of what we have heard during these days following Ash Wednesday: We are stardust, each of us, all of creation. We are all connected—that is the fundamental nature of our reality. We cannot *not* be connected. We are to obey the commandment to choose life, knowing that obedience has to do with listening and responding in freedom and love. Observing the season of Lent offers us the opportunity to see where we have missed the mark, where we have lived from within the illusion that we are separate and apart from others. We begin our observance by rending our hearts, exposing them to ourselves and to God. We continue by asking difficult questions, remaining vulnerable to the God who gently points out our tendency to be superficial and our need to have connections healed, a God eager to offer the quantum grace required for our reconciliation and restoration. Evidence of our transformation, Isaiah has reminded us, will be manifested by release of those bound unjustly, the untying of yokes of oppression, clothing the naked, feeding the hungry, repairing breaches. *Then* light shall rise in our own darkness, and we will be healed.

Reminded of who we are and who we can become, we are ready to pray today's psalm:

> Your ways, O Lord, make known to me;
>> teach me your paths,
>> Guide me in your truth and teach me,
>> for you are God my savior. (Ps 25:4–5)

We know that we need salvation and that it can come only from the Holy One, who is eager to teach and guide us compassionately, kindly, mercifully. On our part, we must engage the grace given—and change.

We need to recall our connectedness to Christ, who contributes to our salvation in two ways. First, Christ is salvation itself, the personification of grace poured out in abundance, the one who entered into the struggle between life and death and emerged triumphant. In Christ the power of the Resurrection is made available to each of us. This is the mystery of our faith, the mystery upon which we stake our lives.

There is a second way that Christ is essential for our salvation. It is the human Jesus who teaches and guides us, who models for us what it is like to live beyond the superficial and in full awareness of the connectedness that is at the heart of life itself. Jesus shows us, through his actions and interactions, how to lean into the grace that is there, how to live connected in a ruptured world, how to respond in cocreative ways to the Holy One who desires only that we choose life.

Where does the human Jesus begin? He goes to the desert, driven there by the Spirit. The desert is a requirement, even for the Son of God. Jesus does not side-step this moment in his life, but appears to embrace it fully. He *remains* there, not by being subjected to any threat, but by staying faithful to divine invitation. It is the human Jesus who experiences Satan's temptations, the human Jesus who responds in a cocreative way, his own volition supported by holy grace.

Temptations—whether we give in to them or not—expose us. They expose our hearts, they rend our hearts, if we let them. In Jesus' own desert experience his heart is rent, his longing exposed, and this opening of his heart seems to prepare him for the mission that is to be his life and his death—and the fulfillment of the covenant established with Noah.

The tale of Noah is significant. Today we hear the end of the narrative, but it is important to remember the whole. God approaches Noah and says, "I have determined to make an end of all flesh, for the earth is filled with violence because of them" (Gn 6:13, NRSV). God then gives Noah instructions to build an ark, and Noah obeys. It is violence that the Holy One abhors, violence the last straw that breaks divine patience and sets God into motion. And what is violence, other than the result of continued and prolonged failure to recognize the connectedness that is our truth?

God is determined to start over again. It is not creation to which God wants to put an end, but the violation of connectedness. The plan involves stripping Earth of everything but the most essential, going down to the bare-boned minimum for survival. God does not negate the pronouncement that creationkind is good and very good (Genesis 1), but insists that the hostility must go.

And what is the bare-boned essential for survival? What remains and becomes the foundation for what comes after? It is connectedness, expressed in relationship: Noah and his wife, their sons and their wives, animals in pairs. No one, nothing, is left without an "other." And the divine Other remains connected to this remnant, sustaining, leading, guiding them as they die to the old and are born into the new.

The story of Noah is appropriate for Lent because it reminds us of our need for salvation, which is nothing more or less than living in connectedness, fully attentive, fully aware of who we are. God's offer of salvation has come time and again, in quantum waves throughout human history, always a cocreative act that involves human effort coupled with divine grace.

To remind Noah and his family—and us—of this truth, God establishes a covenant. The covenant is not a settlement of hostilities with negotiated terms. It is God's fundamental statement of the way things must be. God tells Noah and his family that the covenant is "between me and you and all living creatures." Any plan of salvation that excludes Earth would seem, then, to be a breach of the covenant. Any plan of salvation not based upon and flowing out of connectedness—our connectedness with the Holy One and with one another—will violate the terms of the agreement and lead once again to violence in one form or another.

The story of Noah tells us that salvation, although dependent upon human response, is not only for humankind; it is for "every living creature" with whom we are connected. The establishment of the covenant assures us of God's desire for us to live in a spirit of connectedness.

We are given great gifts—but we also have great responsibility. At the beginning of this Lenten season it is imperative that we ask ourselves about the quality of our connections. Can we, as Jesus demonstrates, remain in a place where we allow a stripping to occur? Can we rend our hearts and keep them open for forty days, just as Jesus did in his desert experience? Can we, like Noah, listen attentively to God's voice, obey the nudging we hear, live in fidelity to all the relationships that are part of our lives, and affirm what old mystics and the new physics tell us, that we are one—all creation? Connectedness is not only the fundamental nature of our reality, but the fulfillment of what it means to be human. That is the covenant we are called to live, the covenant that brings us to life.

For Reflection/Journaling:

- I put into words or an image the covenant I experience in my relationship with God.
- How faithful have I been to the covenant between myself and God? Between myself and all living creatures?
- I remember God's compassion toward me, the times when I have failed in some way, yet God remained faithful and washed away the failure and allowed me to begin again. I allow that compassion to flow throughout my entire being, then extend it to all the relationships in my life.
- I bring my reflection to prayer. . . .

Second Sunday of Lent

(Cycle B)

Scripture Readings:
Genesis 22:1–2, 9a, 10–13, 15–18
Psalm 116
Romans 8:31b–34
Mark 9:2–10

Ready!

This Sunday's readings include two mountaintop experiences. Both have to do with identity and transfiguration. The first reading describes Abraham's journey to Moriah and his response to God's command to sacrifice his only son Isaac. We are told that the experience is a test. Experienced teachers often say that every good test is a lesson in itself, and here there is no exception.

For many years Abraham has been accustomed to conversing with the Holy One. We can sense the connectedness as Abraham responds, "Ready!" when God calls out his name. We know that Abraham has responded obediently since the first invitation that called him to leave the land of Ur and journey to the land promised by God. We also know that Isaac is the tangible evidence of God's promise to make Abraham's descendents as numerous as the stars, the ultimate sign of divine blessing.

It is possible to say that Isaac is what made Abraham Abraham. Isaac's existence testifies to Abraham's identity. He is proof of the promise that his father has heard God clearly and correctly. It is reasonable to imagine that just gazing at his son reminded Abraham that he had come so far—and in so many ways. He must have felt great pleasure as he watched his son mature, growing day by day toward adulthood. Surely Isaac gives Abraham peace, even as he moves closer and closer to his own death.

Imagine how Abraham must have felt when he heard God's message—the one that made no sense at all in light of God's own promise. Surely he had misunderstood! Surely God could not be asking *this*—something not only unspeakable, but unimaginable! Not a token gesture, but a real surrender, a moment of truth that splits Abraham in half and exposes his heart to God.

The story of Abraham is a needed reminder. God's promises are good, but we must watch for the temptation to place the promise above the Holy One who makes the promise. The mystery behind the promise—*that* is the source of our identity. Abraham reminds us that we can become attached not only to sinful ways of living, but to good things as well. And attachment is quite different from connectedness. Attachment, if we look deeply enough, has a hook in egocentric fear. Attachment replaces attentiveness with narrowmindedness. Attachment sucks the life out of connections and depletes relationships. Attachment can focus us in fear rather than center us love. Our identity flows from connectedness—unrestricted connectedness that dispels fear, calls us to gentle awareness, and fills our relationships with freedom and love.

Abraham passes the test. Any tendency toward attachment that may have been in him has been removed. Abraham withholds nothing from God, and God returns the favor. There is a sense in which we can say that Abraham experiences a transfiguration. The word means "to change in shape," "to change in outward form and appearance," "to transform," "to change." The description is certainly applicable to Abraham. After this experience, how can he ever be the same? After having his heart and soul split wide open, how can he ever again resemble his former self? Prepared to give everything he has, his outward appearance must give evidence to the inner transformation. Refusing to hold back his only son, the symbol of his hope and his heart, he gives us a glimpse of what God is like and just how far God will go to save the descendents of Abraham again and again.

The Transfiguration of Jesus is about identity as well. The gospel account depicts a second mountaintop experience. Jesus leads Peter, James, and John away from the others and up a high mountain. He is transfigured before their eyes, and they are terrified as they witness first Jesus' brilliance and then his conversation with Elijah and Moses.

What are we to make of Jesus' connection to these two prophets? What is the point? Often we read the Transfiguration narrative with resurrection and Christ's divinity as our lens. We tend to see the experience as a vision, as it is portrayed in Matthew's gospel. But what if we stay with the humanity of Jesus? What, then, does the connectedness between the human Jesus—a man with a price on his head and whose fate seems clear—and these two prophets signify?

Elijah was filled with the fire of God, the prophet who did not die, but rode into heaven on a flaming chariot. He made no compromise in speaking what God had revealed to him, even while standing alone. He was about truth and justice, compassion and peace. Ever passionate in his service of the Holy One, his heart was filled with faith and always leaned toward the poor.

Moses was a leader and liberator. He was the one God chose to lead the former slaves through the desert and to the Promised Land. Moses was the one who knew how to listen attentively, conveying what he heard to the Israelites and demonstrating patience as they grappled with what it meant to live as chosen and free. Time and again he stood in the breach, one hand extended toward God, the other toward his people, staking a claim in the truth that he knew and lived: in God is justice and mercy, life and love.

What better presence could there be for the human Jesus at this moment in his life? In Elijah he finds a passionate companion and the fire he needs to remain ablaze as conspirators seek to douse his determination. In Moses he encounters a counselor who knows patience and perseverance, and who has experienced the disappointment of not being able to set foot in the place that was the intended destination of his journey. Jesus, at the pinnacle of his mission, needs relationships that sustain him, that keep him connected to his own heart and to his own call. He finds this connectedness in Elijah and Moses.

What is the significance of the Transfiguration for Peter, James, and John? Perhaps they need to see not only Jesus, but his need for connectedness to others and to all that has gone before. Perhaps they need to have affirmed the truth that relationship is primary, that connectedness is what enables us to become all that we can become, all that God calls us to be.

When Jesus comes down from the mountain with Peter, James, and John, he charges them not to tell anyone about what has occurred "except when the Son of Man had risen from the dead." So they keep the matter to themselves, the gospel tells us, questioning what the words mean. They carry the question, live the question, able to do so, no doubt, because they, too, have been changed, transfigured, shaped a bit more fully into the image and likeness of one who was their life.

It is clear that God is the one who invites transfiguration. Many of us have experienced moments of transfiguration, times when we've been called to a mountaintop and asked to become more than we could ever imagine. The question splits us open, calling for sacrifice that we think we cannot make—but we can be assured that through listening and obeying, through being attentive to divine movements and responsive to divine love, we too will be changed. We will be transfigured.

For Reflection/Journaling:

- I consider the difference between "connectedness" and "attachment" and examine how I have experienced each of them in relationships.
- I recall moments of transfiguration that I have experienced—and how they transformed my life and my relationships.
- I bring my reflection to prayer. . . .

Third Sunday of Lent

(Cycle B)

Scripture Redings:
Exodus 20:1–17
Psalm 19
1 Corinthians 1:22–25
John 2:13–25

You shall not have other gods besides me.

The gospel reading for this Sunday of Lent contains an image that few of us forget: an angry Jesus in the temple, whip in hand, overturning the tables of the vendors and money-changers. Coupled with the passage from Exodus that contains God's threat of punishment to the disobedient, we may feel uncomfortable and disturbed, particularly by the latter passage. What are we to make of a God who threatens severe punishment—especially when we recall the story of Noah and how violence was the cause that pushed God to the limit? How do we reconcile these words with what we have come to experience—that the Holy One is a God of mercy and forgiveness?

It is important to recall the milieu in which our scripture was written and to know that while scripture is considered inerrant in matters of faith, we recognize that social conventions have changed as our understanding of humankind has developed. It is necessary to separate divine revelation from cultural convention. For example, slave ownership, mentioned in the passage from Exodus, was normal practice in the ancient world, but today we deplore such a custom and do not use scripture to justify a practice that we know in our hearts is wrong. We must likewise remember that descriptions of God in scripture flow out of that same ancient worldview and that to see God as violent and vengeful goes against our experience and understanding of a God whose nature is love. We continue to affirm God's love of justice, and continue to accept God's discipline, but from within a framework of love, not violence. This kind of awareness allows for growth in our understanding of what it mean to be human—and made in the image and likeness of God—without negating the belief that scripture is inspired. In this way we can revise our understanding of who God is, separating out the cultural conventions, leaving in place the kernels of truth.

To get at the heart of what today's readings are intended to convey, it is helpful to look at them in light of what we have brought to our Lenten reflection thus far: we are stardust, each of us. We are all connected to the Holy One and to one another. We cannot choose *not* to be connected, but we can choose the quality of our connectedness. We have been given the gift of freedom in order to choose well and live responsibly and responsively the life given to us. We are commanded by God to choose life, and choosing anything less than life will lead to death, not as a result of God inflicting punishment, but as the natural consequence of being enslaved to anything less than love. It appears that God's dream for us—a dream echoed in the life and ministry of Jesus—is to live in loving connectedness with one another and all creation. The starting point for such a life is obedience, *ob audire*, which means "to listen." God's dream is that we listen carefully and choose to follow the law that leads to liberation.

The Ten Commandments begin with the introduction that prompts the Israelites' memory: "I . . . am your God, who brought you out of the land of Egypt, that place of slavery." God reminds the people that they have been delivered from captivity through divine intervention. They have been set free, but remain connected to the Holy One who has accompanied and sustained them through the desert. They are who they are and where they are because of their relationship with the Holy One, and this relationship is primary, manifested in their response to God and to one another. The commandments, then, are about maintaining the connectedness that is the source of their life.

It doesn't seem unreasonable to suggest that the first commandment is the most significant, for clear and close adherence to this law will consequently entail adherence to all the others. "You shall have no other gods beside me." How easy it is to dismiss this decree, falling prey to the sin of superficiality again. The voices of the lesser gods are all around us, in our culture, in our hearts, in our attachments and our fears. In a culture of plenty we easily worship at the shrine of materialism. In hearts that can become obsessed by attachments and shrouded in fear, we can bow down to manipulation and control. Long past their usefulness, we can confuse parental voices and egocentric demands with the call to discipline and instruction. And we can do these things in the name of God—a misuse of God and a misunderstanding of humanity.

The purpose of the commandments is to give the Israelites a picture of what living in connectedness looks like, a life in which there is honor and respect within families and among neighbors, where God is reverenced and obeyed through attentive listening and humble response. But the Israelites still seem not to get it. Perhaps this is why the commandment "Remember to keep holy the sabbath day" is necessary. In keeping sabbath, in resting and reflecting and remembering, we are called back, back to the truth of who we are in God, reaffirming the intention to live in the connectedness that gives life.

The gospel scene in the temple, where Jesus drives out those doing business, reminds us that the threat of false gods does not ever go away. Jesus' passion for the one true God makes him keenly aware of how much the people have deviated from the truth and been unfaithful to the relationship with Love. It is not only money-changers and vendors who have strayed into worshiping the false gods of money and possessions. Those who have become accustomed, who no longer notice the infidelity, are culpable as well. Failure to stay in relationship with the God of love who calls us to choose life defiles the temple—not merely the architectural structure, but the temple of flesh that is sacred by virtue of God's presence.

The gospel tells us that Jesus "did not need anyone to testify about human nature. He himself understood it well." Jesus understands how easily we can stray, how effortlessly we can fall into relationships with false gods and false goods. And because he knows that fullness of life comes from no other source than the Holy One, he is vehement in his response to those who systematize and institutionalize anything that leads to a sense of disconnection. He knows that the commandments of God point to life, and life is what we are called to choose.

For Reflection/Journaling:

- What are the false gods that intrigue or entrap me?
- I make today a sabbath, resting, reflecting, remembering, reaffirming what I know to be true about the Holy One.
- I bring my reflection to prayer. . . .

Fourth Sunday of Lent

(Cycle B)

Scripture Readings:
2 Chronicles 36:14–16, 19–23
Psalm 137
Ephesians 2:4–10
John 3:14–21

By the streams of Babylon we sat and wept when we remembered Zion.

Out of compassion God "early and often" has sent messengers to Israel, but the prophets go unheeded as the people add infidelity to infidelity. Israel has a history of scoffing at the message and mocking the messenger. They refuse to listen and obey, refuse to remain in the shelter of God's love and protection. Their contaminated spirits give rise to abominations, and eventually the chosen ones who have been led out of slavery fall prey to their enemies once again.

Exile was a tactic used by a conqueror who wanted to insure that there would be no uprising from the defeated. Leaders, artisans, anyone who might be inclined to organize resistance, were taken captive and forced to reside in the land of the enemy. The method was intended to separate the captives, to dilute their commitment to their own customs and beliefs, and to break their resolve to remember who they were. Exile meant that the voices they heard, the customs they were forced to honor, the laws they were compelled to observe were cruel reminders that their freedom had been forfeited and that they were not at home. For the faithful, the experience was bitter, a painful estrangement that robbed them of dignity and joy. We can hear the suffering in the heart-wrenching words of the psalmist:

By the streams of Babylon
we sat and wept
when we remembered Zion. (Ps 137:1)

As distressing as exile is, there is a worse state, mentioned in the passage from Ephesians: to be "dead in our transgressions." To be dead is to lose memory. To be dead is to have no awareness of what is lost, no recollection of the meaning of suffering, no recall of what it means to live in dignity and joy. The loss of geographic location is small in comparison to the loss of belonging in and to the Holy One. Nothing short of quantum grace is required to restore the connection. And quantum grace is available for those who seek it.

How is such a thing possible if one is dead in transgression and exiled from God and self? Perhaps Nicodemus gives us a clue. He has come to Jesus in the night, sensing both his inner darkness and his longing for light. When Jesus tells him he must be born from above, he asks "How can a person once grown old be born again?"—another seemingly impossible state of affairs. Nicodemus hears the most wonderful news. "For God so loved the world" that salvation has not only come but is standing before him in the person of Jesus. In the person of Jesus his memory of who he is and who God is gets stirred. In the person of Jesus he gets a grasp of the possibility of Paradise.

Like any birth, being born from above will require a death of some kind. It will mean having to die to our sins, those places in our lives where we consistently miss the mark. It will mean having to let go of superficiality, daring to continue to live with a rent, vulnerable heart. It will involve listening attentively and responding faithfully. It will mean living the truth, not merely assenting to it. Jesus tells Nicodemus, "whoever lives the truth comes to the light." Living the truth brings us to fullness of life.

Early and often messages have come, not just to the Israelites, but to each of us. The messages are in scripture, they are in our relationships, they are in our faith-filled traditions, they are in our hearts. If we listen carefully, we will hear the prophetic voice within that urges us to connect to love, connect in love—and connected, no land will ever be foreign, no darkness will ever overcome the light.

For Reflection/Journaling:

- I recall a time of personal darkness or exile. Did it cause me to weep? What was it that was lost or displaced in me?
- I remember a time of return. I sit in the experience, recalling my feelings and thoughts about once again being "home."
- I bring my reflection to prayer. . . .

Fifth Sunday of Lent

(Cycle B)

Scripture Readings:
Jeremiah 31:31–34
Psalm 51
Hebrews 5:7–9
John 12:20–33

Unless a grain of wheat falls to the ground and dies,
it remains just a grain of wheat.

God has a dream.

In God's dream, life will differ from that lived under the old covenant. In this dream the Holy One will not have to take the Israelites by the hand and lead them forth from the land of Egypt where "I had to show myself their master." In God's dream the law will be in their hearts, and "I will be their God, and they shall be my people." God will possess the chosen ones, and the chosen ones will possess God—a possession characterized by love, for that is the heart of the law, and by presence that fulfills the longing of all hearts, both human and divine. Living the dream will be an experience of connectedness in which the capacity to choose life is the norm and the energy for loving relationship is standard. But God's dream has been deferred time and again simply because the Holy One who sacrifices the Son will not sacrifice our freedom.

There is nothing more compelling than love. And there is no more compelling love than that of the Holy One and of Jesus, the one we have come to know as the Christ. It seems that the love of God is utterly irresistible, yet we continue to refuse or delay our response to the offer. In our fear, do we think something better may come along? Or do we simply fear the fulfillment of the longing—both God's and ours—because of what it might entail?

Stories that flow out of human experiences of war or natural disasters often affirm what is an essential part of the human spirit—a propensity toward self-preservation and survival. Instinctively we struggle against death and overcome great suffering to emerge *alive*. It often seems that when we are in the greatest danger of losing our lives, our capacity to withstand threat and overcome every peril comes to the fore.

This instinct for survival, wonderful gift that it is, becomes a great obstacle when it comes to our salvation—and the fulfillment of God's dream. In the gospel Jesus tells us that "unless a grain of wheat falls to the ground and dies, it remains just a grain of wheat." Without death, there is no transformation. Without death, there is no fruit. As paradoxical as it sounds, without death, we die.

What Jesus asks of us goes against our fundamental nature—to *choose* to die. Even when we give assent, we resist instinctively. We may give in to a transition here and there, hoping that gradual change may forestall a sudden death. But what Jesus talks about is not any gradual transition that is merely uncomfortable. What he intends is a definitive, painful death that removes all traces of a former egocentric self. No wonder we run.

For Jesus, his death is related to the glorification of God. To glorify means to reveal the hidden nature of someone. Jesus' death will glorify the Holy One, it will reveal who God is: the divine dreamer and lover who longs to live in relationship. God will glorify Jesus as well, that all may come to recognize that this indeed is the Word made flesh, the Beloved of God. The revelation of all that is hidden comes through death, and no other way.

And so Jesus shows us what to do. He becomes the seed that chooses to die. He tells the disciples that his hour has come. His passion has begun, and he will model for us what we must do if we want to take part in the dream. Planted in the soil of divine love, the seed dies, but the fruit that follows is exquisite, giving death a fullness of meaning beyond words. But the seed that is Jesus also gets planted in us. If our hearts are closed, will the seed find a place to lodge? If we say yes to the seed and to the death of our own egocentricity and fear, then the seed that lodges in us will root in us, able not only to grow and bear fruit, but to become seed as well. As we become seed for others, we join with Jesus in a cocreative process that transforms our own lives and the world.

God has a dream. Do we choose to enter into the process—one that involves dying—that makes the dream come true?

For Reflection/Journaling:

- I imagine what life will be like when God's dream comes true.

- How do I hinder God's dream? How do I help bring it about?
- Where am I being called to die? How do I resist? How do I say yes?
- I bring my reflection to prayer. . . .

Passion/Palm Sunday

(Cycle B)

Scripture Readings:
    Mark 11:1–10 (The Procession with Palms)
    Isaiah 50:4–7
    Psalm 22
    Philippians 2:6–11
    Mark 14:1–15:47

Crucify him! Crucify him!

In most of our liturgies for Passion Sunday there is a procession—if not of the whole congregation, then of representatives of the assembly. The procession is highly symbolic, reenacting Jesus' entrance into Jerusalem on the back of a colt, announcing that the reign of God is *now*, if we choose, and challenging those who are opposed to the reign to come out in open opposition to the person and message of Jesus. But we must not allow the symbolic gesture to end here. This week that we call Holy is about our journey as well, and this procession is our entrance into the week and the process of transformation that Jesus' passion, death, and resurrection signifies. We are not invited to be bystanders this week, but active participants in the Mystery that defines who we are.

The readings from Isaiah and Philippians are the same for each of the cycles. In the passage from Isaiah, we readily recognize Jesus: "God has given me a well-trained tongue, that I might know how to speak to the weary a word that will rouse them." Yes, this is the Jesus we know. Isaiah goes on: "Morning after morning [God] opens my ear that I may hear." Yes, we know how obedient Jesus is to the Word. We know of Jesus' fidelity to prayer and his passion for healing ruptured connections. "I have not rebelled, have not turned back. I gave my back to those who beat me, my cheeks to those who plucked my beard; my face I did not shield from buffets and spitting." This reminds us of the humiliation Jesus experienced at the hands of his persecutors and the cruelty of his death. He lived a life of connectedness to God, a life of radical love and uncompromising freedom. And living this way cost him his life.

But we must also recall that the scripture readings during these weeks of Lent have called us to obedience, to living connected to love and to growing in our capacity to be free. We, too, as disciples, ought to be able to claim, at least partially, "God has given me a well-trained tongue." As disciples, we too must speak a rousing word to the weary. Our mornings ought to find us listening, asking God to open our ears and our hearts, not rebelling, not turning back from the truth that has grasped us. Authentic discipleship will have its cost. Like Jesus, we will recognize that "God is my help, therefore I am not disgraced," and we will set our faces like flint, not because we have willed it, but because the God of quantum grace wills us to be part of the divine dream for all creation.

The passage from Philippians reminds us of the great love of God. It was God who chose to enter into human life, laying aside any semblance of divinity, becoming fully human. I remember asking students how to explain the mystery of the Incarnation—what it means when we say that Jesus is both human and divine. Invariably someone would state that Jesus is "fifty-fifty," meaning fifty percent human and fifty percent divine. But that's not how Christianity defines Jesus. We say that he is *fully* human and *fully* divine—one hundred percent of each. This is the great mystery of our faith, that the fullness of God entered fully into humanity. This was God's dream all along—to be one with us. In Jesus we behold God's dream in the flesh and are invited to enter into the dream as well. What humility God has, and how the recognition of God's humility humbles us.

The Passion narrative can be understood on multiple levels. It is a story of cosmic significance, the great battle of good versus evil. We witness the coming together of systemic forces in a way that turns deadly. Those involved in the conspiracy against Jesus expose the ugliness of intentional evil-doing. They live in the illusion that they are separate and set apart from their constituents. The central focus of their lives is a distorted notion of the law that places restrictive loads on the backs of those who are already heavily burdened.

The Passion story also includes those guilty of sins of omission. Pilate knows precisely what the conspirators are up to, yet he refuses to exercise his power and declines to intervene. He prefers to play it safe, to appease the religious officials who use poorly the little power they do have. Entrenched in an unjust system of his own, Pilate simply does nothing and stands back to watch the atrocity unfold.

The crowd has its part to play as well. The same folk who earlier waved palm branches as Jesus rode into Jerusalem, thinking that their liberation had come in the way they had expected it to come, now cry out, "Crucify him! Crucify him!" Unable to hear on their own, they are dissuaded by those who are listening to the voice of evil. They, too, are guilty. The sin of superficiality—having ears but not hearing, having eyes but not seeing, allowing others to tell them what to think and feel—serves evil intentions as much as the sins of commission and omission perpetrated by the other conspirators.

When we do not choose to live in connectedness, when we do not choose to listen with a vulnerable heart, we, too, become participants in the suffering of others. Intentional evil, appeasement and indifference, superficiality and refusing to live responsibly out of our freedom all combine with deadly consequences—not only for Jesus as we remember his Passion, but for all creation. We have only to look around us, and we will see it everywhere.

In Peter we see someone who tries not to fall into the heart of evil, who strives to live in connectedness. His eyes and ears and heart have been opened by the words and love of Jesus. He has come to believe that Jesus is the Messiah, but he, too, has misunderstood the dream, even while trying to embrace it. "The spirit is willing, but the flesh is weak," Jesus tells him. Indeed. Peter wills to live connected, but he does not understand that connectedness, the fundamental truth of our reality, is a gift to be received and cannot be brought about by even the best-intentioned will. This is Peter's lesson as he works through the experience of denial. Living connected in and through love is not something we can do on our own, even when we desire it with all our hearts. Living connected in and through love requires quantum grace—a great act of grace, an outpouring of grace such as creation has not seen before.

Jesus is this grace outpoured. His life and death show us how readily available is divine grace. His life and death also show us that as cocreators we must participate in the process. We must assent to love. And it seems that the assent to love always induces fear to raise its ugly head. It is fear that has motivated all the evil we see unfolding. Fear. It is fear that prompts us to sell our freedom and become its slave. It is fear that lies to us and tells us that the dream is impossible.

What we see in Jesus as he is questioned by the Sanhedrin and Pilate, what we see in the one who gives his back to those who beat him and his face to those who buffet him, is fearlessness. Jesus dies, but fear dies first. After Gethsemane, it is not to be found in him. Perhaps this is why we affirm the divinity of his nature even here, before the Resurrection, for to see a human being with no trace of fear truly is divine.

The Passion is about Jesus, to be sure, but it is about us as well. Like a parable, this narrative questions us, exposes us, then offers a glimpse of truth and the grace to embrace it. May we allow our hearts to be questioned, remaining rent during this Holy Week, so that we may be prepared for the transformative dying and rising that is to take place within us.

For Reflection/Journaling:

- I examine the fear in my life and how it contributes to suffering.
- I imagine myself without a trace of fear.
- I ask for God to open my ear, that I might hear—and then I listen.
- I bring my reflection to prayer. . . .

First Sunday of Lent

(Cycle C)

Scripture Readings:
Deuteronomy 26:4–10
Psalm 91
Romans 10:8–13
Luke 4:1–13

The word is near you. . . .

As we enter into the readings of the first Sunday of Lent, let us remember that on Ash Wednesday we were signed with ashes and acknowledged that we are dust—stardust, part of the great mystery of connectedness that is essential to all creation. This connectedness is the fundamental nature of our reality, and our scriptures record how the Holy One continues to call us back to the awareness of the unity that underpins all of life.

The weekday readings have called us to choose life, affirming our freedom and responsibility to act cocreatively with God. We have been reminded that the kind of fasting that the Holy One desires is this: to release those unjustly bound, to untie those who are yoked, to set free the oppressed, to share bread with the hungry, and to shelter the homeless, to clothe the naked and not turn our backs on our own. In other words, we are to repair connections that have been ruptured, whether through intentional actions or neglect. If we resist the sin of superficiality, we will recognize our own culpability and the ways we fail to use our cocreative power to set others—and ourselves—free. Although the task can seem enormously difficult, we are asked to heal the oppression of those *in our midst*, becoming part of an organic process of healing and cocreation that can return creationkind to its intended unity.

Today's readings begin with Moses speaking to the Israelites, reminding them of the manner in which they are to bring their offerings to God. They are to recall their history, their connectedness to the God who has been with them since the time of Abram, the God who has been with them in slavery in Egypt, who arranged their release with "terrifying power, with signs and wonders," and who accompanied them across the desert from captivity to "this land flowing with milk and honey." In presenting the first fruits from their own soil to the Holy One, the Israelites are to continue to remember, continue to be grateful for all that God has done for them.

The reading from Romans echoes the passage from Deuteronomy in which God speaks to the people through Moses as they prepare to enter the Promised Land:

> For this commandment which I enjoin on
> you today is not too mysterious and remote
> for you. It is not up in the sky, that you
> should say, "Who will go up in the sky to get
> it for us and tell us of it, that we may carry it
> out? . . . No, it is something very near to you,
> already in your mouths and in your hearts;
> you have only to carry it out. (Dt 30:11–14)

The word that we are to heed is in our hearts—very near, although sometimes it feels inaccessible. During the season of Lent we are invited and challenged to attend to what is in our hearts. We are asked to return to the awareness of the connectedness that lies beneath all of life, recognizing not only that there is to be no distinction between Jew and Greek, but that there is to be no disconnection among any of us, no matter how we name or label ourselves.

Jesus is the one who listens to the word that resides in his heart, and Jesus is the one who requires us to do the same, so that the reign of God may move from being an impossible dream to an everyday reality. In this season we are reminded how very difficult the dream is, how very easy it is to stray from sincere intentions. As the gospel reading shows, there are forces at work that seek to disempower us, to pull us off track and push us into taking shortcuts. Jesus says "no" to anything that disengages his own life and ministry from the life and love of the Holy One. There are no shortcuts for him, and there can be none for us. We, too, must enter the desert of our hearts and be confronted by the adversary who waits for us there.

The desert experience is terrifying, for it strips us of our illusions and exposes our egocentricity. But as frightening as confrontation with our temptations may be, the occasion provides an opportunity to receive the grace that is ever present and ever available. If we welcome the grace, we may leave our desert with greater strength and resolve, empowered by the Spirit and set on a course that will not only bring about our own transformation, but the transformation of the world.

And so here, at the beginning of Lent, we look at the temptation of Jesus. Since temptation is part of the process of transformation for the human Jesus, we must expect that it will be part of our process as well. It is the Holy Spirit who lures Jesus into the desert, where all kinds of spirits are known to roam. Satan appears, making every effort to entice Jesus to compromise body, mind, and spirit.

Famished after a lengthy fast, Jesus is tempted to turn stone to bread, to allow his stomach to take precedence over his heart. Mindful of his gifts and attentive to his call, Jesus is tempted to use his gifts and abort his call in the service of egocentricity—for the promise of power and glory that are disconnected from the divine. Finally, with both Jesus and the Evil One aware of the power of the Spirit within Jesus, Jesus is tempted to abuse the power that has been given to him by the Holy One, to abuse the relationship with the spirit world to serve his own purposes. Jesus rejects each shortcut, each enticement to allow egocentricity to set the agenda or the course.

Jesus' own experience in the desert poses significant questions for us. Satan tempted Jesus to turn stone to bread. In our culture we rarely fast in any significant way, nor do we experience the deprivation of nourishment that is a way of life for most people of our planet. Perhaps it is difficult for us to imagine the depth of hunger that comes from physically abstaining from food for an extended period of time. But we do hunger. Sometimes it seems that our appetite for "things" is insatiable, and we must ask ourselves, "What is my hunger?" What do I long for most—and where do I get sidetracked, giving in to a lesser hunger?

Satan tempts Jesus with a distorted "power and glory" that is disconnected from the divine. Where do I manifest a desire for the manipulative control and unwarranted attention that flow out of self-absorption? Finally, in tempting Jesus to throw himself from the parapet of the temple and be rescued by angels, Satan is tempting Jesus to test God. He wants Jesus to ask the Holy One to be in the service of egocentricity rather than genuine truth and love. How many times do my own prayers do the same—asking, even tempting, the Holy One to respond to my self-centered desires, which in effect asks God not to be the God of truth and love?

The questions are difficult because the temptation is real, striking at the heart of who we are and who God is, but they are an essential part of the process of learning to listen to our heart. Our temptations are to be recognized and named, so that we may travel less hindered on the path of love that will bring the reign of God into a world that needs to know now, above all else, that we are all connected, we are all one.

For Reflection/Journaling:

- What are the temptations that prevent me from choosing life and living out of the gifts and call that have been given to me? I ask God to teach me how to respond.
- I recall a time that I have been given the grace to overcome temptation. I feel the empowerment that came from that resistance.
- I bring my reflection to prayer. . . .

Second Sunday of Lent

(Cycle C)

Scripture Readings:
   Genesis 15:5–12, 17–18
   Psalm 27
   Philippians 3:17–4:1
   Luke 9:28b–36

Look up at the sky and count the stars, if you can.

Long ago, on a crisp winter night while I was still a college student, I had an experience that remains unforgettable. After a long day of study, I decided to take a walk. Stepping out of the dorm and walking through a parking lot, I looked up. There, strewn across the dark sky, was an incredibly beautiful array of stars, flickering like tiny fires, filling the sky as far as my eyes could see. I was caught up, overwhelmed by the sense that I was part of a vast mystery of life, a mystery that I could never understand, a mystery from which I could never extricate myself, even if I tried. All my questions about the existence of the divine dissolved in that moment, dispersed, thrown across the universe, just like the stars.

This is the experience I often recall when I read today's passage from Genesis. God takes Abram outside and says, "Look up at the sky and count the stars, if you can." I wonder, was Abram overwhelmed by the mystery? Caught up by the sight of the tiny fires that flickered as far as he could see, were his deepest questions swept away? Could he do nothing other than say yes to the God who was irresistible mystery—and who invited him to become part of that mystery as well? As Abram looks up, God reveals a little more of Godself to Abram: "I am the Lord who brought you from Ur of the Chaldeans to give you this land as a possession." In this moment, in this place under the stars, the Holy One makes a covenant with Abram, a promise of fidelity and love that will surpass the mystery and magnificence of the stars suspended above his head. It is a moment that begins to transform and transfigure the man known as the father of three religious traditions.

The covenant, we know, is breached time and again by its human participants. During the week we read the story of Jonah, the reluctant, run-away prophet who liked to be considered one of the chosen, but who didn't necessarily like the responsibility that came with it. And in his letter to the Philippians, Paul reminds the believers to "stand firm," not conducting themselves like those whose God is their stomach and whose end is destruction. Always it appears necessary for God to call humankind back, to remind us once again of the covenant—and who we are.

Jesus knows who he is. He knows that he has a unique relationship with the Holy One, and he knows that his life has no meaning separated from the divine reality. He has rejected the temptation to be less than who he is—fully human, fully attentive. Jesus lives out of this fullness, open to the Mystery that is at the heart of all creation.

The story of the Transfiguration affirms Jesus' identity and allows us to see how the Holy One provides the kind of companioning presence Jesus needs at this moment in his life. As he goes up the mountain to pray, he invites Peter, John, and James to come with him. Luke describes a mystical experience in which the face of Jesus changes in appearance and his clothing becomes "dazzling white." In this moment we see Jesus the prophet in the light of two great prophets.

Moses and Elijah appear and begin to converse with Jesus. In this account, the prophets speak about the "exodus [Jesus] is going to accomplish in Jerusalem." We associate the first exodus with Moses, who led the Israelites out of Egyptian captivity. Passover, the setting for the new exodus that is about to occur, was first celebrated under the leadership of Moses, who had his own mountaintop experience in which Yahweh spoke to him: "I am the God of your father, the God of Abraham, the God of Isaac, and the God of Jacob" (Ex 3:6). The appearance of Moses is a reminder of Yahweh's ongoing revelation and abiding presence, the law and the grace that are the means of salvation.

The Israelites are once again in captivity. Though living under Roman occupation, their slavery goes much deeper. Through their negligence of God's revelation and abiding presence, through failing to grasp the heart of the law and the healing power of grace, they are once again enslaved. Jesus, the new Moses, will begin a new Passover in which he himself is the sacrificial lamb, hoping to call his people to remember who they really are.

Elijah began his prophetic ministry during a time when the Davidic monarchy had descended into wickedness. Having turned their backs on the law and the people, the kings had become instruments of tyranny, oppressing the ones they were obliged to lead and protect. During the reign of King Ahab, Elijah, on Yahweh's command, initiated a major confrontation with the king and his wife Jezebel, who employed four hundred and fifty prophets of Baal as consultants. Yahweh, the true God, consumed the offering of Elijah, while that of the prophets of Baal remained untouched, exposing the false prophets, false rulers, false gods.

Jesus, whose words and deeds have served the truth, is about to enter into a major confrontation himself, one in which the religious rulers charged with the care of the Jewish people will be exposed. They have been false rulers serving false notions of God, laying their lies and deceit on the backs of the people, burdens that no one ought to carry.

Moses and Elijah are fitting companions for Jesus in this crisis of his life, but the narrative tells us that Peter, John, and James are witnesses as well. What significance do the two prophets have for them—and for us? Moses reminds us of the burden of captivity and enslavement that can creep unobtrusively into our lives. His presence nudges us to ask: To what are we enslaved—and how comfortable have we become in our captivity? Where do we fail to heed the law that is written on our hearts, the commandments designed to help us live and grow in freedom?

Elijah's appearance suggests to us that there are times when fiery confrontation with falsehood is necessary. What are the falsehoods, the lies and illusions that ensnare us and cause us to miss the mark? Both prophets remind us that we have a God who desires to be in relationship with us and who longs to pour out quantum grace, that we might live in freedom of heart and remember, for the sake of all creation, who we are.

For Reflection/Journaling:

- I imagine myself climbing to a mountaintop, conversing with Jesus, with Moses and Elijah, with Peter, John, and James. I listen.
- I remember a time in which I have been called to confrontation with what is false. I consider my response.
- I recall an experience in which I experienced a "transfiguration" of my own.
- I bring my reflection to prayer. . . .

Third Sunday of Lent

(Cycle C)

Scripture Readings:
  Exodus 3:1–8a, 13–15
  Psalm 103
  1 Corinthians 10:1–6, 10–12
  Luke 13:1–9

He came in search of fruit, but found none.

God is never in a hurry. Even when the need is urgent, the Holy One doesn't rush, but manifests as a divine Patience that allows us freedom to learn hard lessons and discover the truth through the mistakes we have made. During the weekday readings we have heard the waiting God speak through Isaiah, "Come now, let us set things right" (Is 1:18). And through the parable of the Prodigal Son we have been reminded of God's compassionate love that is ready to forgive, eager for our return, and prepared to greet us with open arms. God is Patience.

In the first reading today we are reminded of God's patience with the Israelites who have lived in slavery for generations. God waits for them to tire of their captivity, waits for them to reclaim their identity and relationship as God's chosen ones. Moses, exiled from the Egyptian palace where he was once known as prince, now lives as an Israelite, a sheepherder who tends his father-in-law's flock. As Moses approaches Horeb, the mountain of God, he sees a flaming bush that is surprisingly not consumed as it burns. Curious, Moses comes closer. A voice cries out from the bush, "Moses! Moses!" Hearing the voice, Moses responds, "Here I am."

Standing on holy ground, Moses listens: "I am the God of Abraham, the God of Isaac, the God of Jacob," Yahweh tells him. "I have witnessed the affliction of my people in Egypt and have heard their cry of complaint against their slave drivers, so I know well what they are suffering." God desires to rescue the people from slavery and lead them to a land of their own, one that flows with milk and honey. The Israelites are ready for release, and Moses, the one who knows how to listen and obey, is the one God has chosen to lead them.

In the letter to the Corinthians, Paul reminds believers to remember their connectedness to those who have gone before. Their ancestors lived under the desert cloud, passed through the sea, ate and drank in an unfriendly land. An entire generation wandered the desert and did not see the Promised Land, not because their destination was so far away, but because their obstinacy was so deeply ingrained. In the desert the Holy One wanted them to recognize their utter dependence upon divine providence, their complete connectedness to God and to one another, and the patient fidelity of the One who desires nothing but relationships joined in and through love.

The parable of the fig tree also tells of God's patience. The story comes after Jesus encounters those who were discussing the latest news. The blood of some Galileans has been spilled by Pilate, and eighteen people have been crushed to death by a falling tower. Because the crowd's interpretation seems to lean toward judgment of the victims, Jesus begins to address them. In regard to the Galileans, Jesus asks. "Do you think that because these Galileans suffered in this way they were greater sinners than all other Galileans?" He continues, "Do you think [those killed by the falling tower] were more guilty than everyone else who lived in Jerusalem?" In order to dispel what is illusion, Jesus confronts the common belief that misfortune and tragedy are signs of God's punishment.

It is to these listeners that Jesus tells the parable. A fig tree is growing in the middle of an orchard (some translations say a vineyard)—that is, it is not in its proper "home." A fig tree, by nature, requires patience, taking several years to bear fruit. It has greedy roots that spread wider than its canopy, so it often invades the root systems of other plants, stealing water and nutrients from the soil around them.

We learn that it is the owner who has had the tree planted in the orchard. What was his purpose? Was it an experiment, a whim? Isn't he a bit ridiculous in his expectations? Yet he is persuaded by the gardener to give the tree another season, at the risk of depleting the soil. How foolish! As a matter of fact, does the gardener not resemble another foolish person we recently encountered in Luke's gospel—the father of the prodigal son, the one who waits and waits for his son to come home, to bear fruit once again after a season of no production? Both the father and the gardener are patient beyond expectation—we might say foolishly so—because they dream of growth in places where others normally give up. Such is the patience of the Holy One.

But there is a difference between this parable and that of the prodigal son. There is an urgency here that the other narrative lacks. While it affirms a patience that goes beyond what is expected, it also holds before us the thought that there will still come a time of reckoning. Patience that awaits growth is held in tension with expectation that counts on a harvest. Jesus uses the parable to warn his listeners that the time is coming—and soon—when they will be held accountable for the kind of harvest they yield.

The gospel also reminds us of God's patience. Like the crowd speaking with Jesus, we can be filled with false beliefs and fail to see the truth. Like the fig tree in the orchard, we can fail to bear fruit even after caring cultivation. Moses teaches us what is essential: listening, attending to the voice of God, recognizing that wherever we stand God is present. God is patient and supportive as we grow in the capacity to use these gifts, ready to offer the grace, but intent upon our bearing fruit.

For Reflection/Journaling:

- I reflect upon a time when I stood on holy ground and heard God's voice.
- I recall an experience of bearing good fruit in due season. I allow the empowerment of that experience to come to me once again.
- I bring my reflection to prayer. . . .

Fourth Sunday of Lent

(Cycle C)

Scripture Readings:
 Joshua 5:9a, 10–12
 Psalm 34
 2 Corinthians 5:17–21
 Luke 15:1–3, 11–32

Whoever is in Christ is a new creation.

Last Sunday we read the parable of the fig tree and considered the consequences of not bearing fruit in due time.
This Sunday we are presented with images that depict what
it is like to reap the harvest. In the passage from Joshua we
hear God speak words to the Israelites, confirming that a
time of blessing has indeed begun: "Today I have removed
the reproach of Egypt from you." The desert lies behind
them, and they share a final Passover meal of manna. After
that, the scripture goes on to say, "No longer was there
manna for the Israelites, who that year ate of the yield of the

land of Canaan." No longer wandering, the Israelites are home in the Promised Land—the land of freedom, the land that has been chosen for them by God.

Clearly this is a time of celebration for the Hebrew people. The lessons of the desert have been difficult, because the desert itself is difficult. There have been moments of grumbling and resistance along the way, but there also have been times of gratitude and obedience. Finally, after a generation has passed, a new people, shaped and formed by their desert experience, comes into a new land, one that flows with milk and honey, promise and hope. Through an experience that can be described as quantum grace, the Israelites once again live with a sense of wholeness and connectedness.

We have followed the former slaves throughout the desert during this season of Lent. And we have dared to look at our own places of captivity, our own enslavement and grumbling and resistance. Like the Israelites, we too have been called back to the covenant, examining the painful breaches we have caused or experienced, noticing and confessing our infidelity, holding on in hope of God's mercy and forgiveness. The reading from Second Corinthians reminds us that our hope is not in vain. "Whoever is in Christ is a new creation: the old things have passed away; behold, new things have come." In Christ we experience a new sense of connection with God and with others. The old things—our faults and failings, our selfishness and tendency toward superficiality—pass away and we become renewed. The new things—healthy connections, living in freedom, assuming our rightful roles as cocreators—are possible through the life and death and resurrection of the one we know as the Christ. The reproach from our own Egypts has been removed, and we will eat of the produce of our own promised land.

We are part of a process, Paul tells us, a process in which the world is being reconciled to God in Christ. The trespasses that have ruptured connections are no longer counted against us, and we are entrusted with the message that will save us all. When we are reconciled, we are re-connected. When we are reconciled, we are forgiven. When we are reconciled, we remember who we are and what our life is about. Like the Israelites, we can rejoice, for the dreams that we dared to dream in slavery have now come true. And now we can help the dream become truth for others, for we have been empowered to become reconcilers ourselves. Like the psalmist, we too can sing, "I will bless the Lord at all times, with praise ever in my mouth."

All this wonder and joy comes about because our God is very much like the foolish father who will not give up on his son. The parable of the Prodigal Son is so familiar that we often fail to hear it. The story is one of incarnation, that place of intersection where divinity is enfleshed and enters into human life. Jesus uses the parable to say to us, "This is what God is like." It is a portrait of infinite compassion, complete and unconditional love, patient waiting, forgiving welcome, and the impulse to connect and embrace.

We are moved by the image of the father receiving the son who returns after squandering wealth and dignity. But the return at the end of the story is made possible by the choices made as it began—with a letting go that must have wrenched the heart of the father who was beyond the naïveté that held his son. Parents know how difficult it is to let go of their children, to allow them to venture out into the world, no matter what their age or how well prepared they seem to be. Loaded with youthful illusions and self-assured ego, they confidently take their leave of us old fools. Even when we know that this is the usual procedure, it is difficult to let go, to allow our children to make their own mistakes, or, what's perhaps more difficult, to allow them to make some of the same mistakes we made. But when we try to control the process, love suffers. And so in love, we surround them with prayer, let go, and watch over them as they walk away.

My sons have been on their own for some time now, and they are learning the lessons that will shape and fashion their becoming. Their leave-takings were on good terms and received our parental blessing. Still, my heart leaps when I hear one of them come through the door and call out, "Hello?" I can only imagine the joy the father in the parable must know when he sees his son coming down the path. And this, Jesus tells us, is how God is. This is how God loves. This is how the Holy One who gifts us with freedom lets us go. And this is the kind of welcome we can expect when we make our returns—open arms, celebration, joy.

As a story of incarnation, the Prodigal Son is also a story about being human. Besides telling us what God is like, Jesus is saying, "This is who you are, too." There is something in our hearts that connects with the father, that identifies with him on a very human level. From our own experience of loving and being loved, we understand what it means to wait with longing and to welcome with open arms. At our best, when we are connected and filled with grace, this is who we are. Each of us has the capacity to love. Each of us has the capacity to let go, to set free, to empower. Each of us has the capacity to welcome, to receive, to restore. This is the life of reconciliation Paul wrote about. This is the life of love Christ calls us to live. This is who we are in Christ— "new creations," welcomed and restored, then set free and empowered to love.

For Reflection/Journaling:

- I get in touch with the ways that I am like the loving father in the parable of the prodigal son.
- I recall a time of having to let go of something or someone I loved. What empowerment came to me as a result?
- I recall a time of return, when I was welcomed, renewed, restored.
- I bring my reflection to prayer. . . .

Fifth Sunday of Lent

(Cycle C)

Scripture Readings:
   Isaiah 43:16–21
   Psalm 126
   Philippians 3:8–14
   John 8:1–11

See, I am doing something new!

It is easy to get caught up in the past, to allow its energy to envelop us and its pain to control who we are. Isaiah's words are addressed to a people in exile, to those who have been cut off from their land and who dream of returning home. Intended to be words of encouragement and promise, they extend hope to those who are tempted to be hopeless. God is not asking the Hebrew people to forget what God has done, for the words themselves allude to these things. They are from the one "who opens a way in the sea and a path in the mighty waters, who leads out chariots and horsemen, a powerful army, till they lie prostrate together, never to rise" (Is 43:16–17).

It is significant that the words of the scripture are in the present tense. God is not only the one who long ago opened the sea of deliverance and wiped out a powerful army. God is the one who *continues* to open paths, who continues to show the way, who continues to be a companioning presence in the now of their lives. "Remember not the events of the past, the things of long ago consider not." God wants their attention to be in the present moment, noticing the now. "See, I am doing something new!" the Holy One says. "Now it springs forth, do you not perceive it?" The words are filled with anticipation and promise. God is hovering, acting, stirring. The Hebrews need to be in the present moment if they are to participate in the unfolding.

The Apostle Paul knows about staying in the present moment. We recall that he was the one who held the cloaks of those who stoned Stephen. His personal mission had been to eradicate the new sect of believers who were known as followers of the Way—until that day when the risen Christ's lightning-bolt visit changed everything. For Paul, nothing holds meaning now except his faith in Christ. Forgetting what lies behind and straining forward to what lies ahead, he has perceived what God is doing and becomes a vital part of the "something new."

The scribes and Pharisees are not so open. Something new is springing forth right in front of them, but they cannot perceive it. As Jesus teaches the crowd who has gathered in the temple area, some scribes and Pharisees burst onto the scene, dragging in a woman who has been caught in adultery. They tell Jesus she has been caught in the very act. "Now in the law," they tell him, "Moses commanded us to stone such a woman. So what do you say?" They are putting Jesus to the test. He speaks no reply, but bends down and begins to write on the ground with his finger. He is putting them to the test.

We will always wonder what Jesus writes. Whatever the words are, it seems to expose the illusion that they have no connection to the woman. Whether they have slept with this woman or not, they have used her for their own impure purposes. They, too, are guilty of their own kind of adultery. One by one, beginning with the elders, they exit the temple, leaving the woman alone with Jesus. Although she, too, is guilty of sin, she alone will hear the words of promise and hope. "Woman, where are they? Has no one condemned you?" No, but they have condemned themselves. "Neither do I condemn you. Go, and from now on do not sin any more." Unlike her accusers, she exits the temple without condemnation and with the sense of liberation that comes from forgiveness.

The readings today tell us that our past and our sins are not nearly as significant as our awareness of God's presence. In God's presence we are healed. In God's presence we are set free from enslavement to worldly things. In God's presence we become open to the Holy One's desire for us to be whole. In God's presence we experience the connectedness that holds us together in love. In God's presence we can hear the joy of the Holy One who speaks to our hearts, "See, I am doing something new!"

For Reflection/Journaling:

- I recall a time in which I was stuck in the past—in my thinking, my memories, my habits, etc.
- I notice an invitation to "something new" that is springing forth before me. I also notice my response to anything "new."
- I bring my reflection to prayer. . . .

Passion/Palm Sunday

(Cycle C)

Scripture Readings:
Luke 19:28–40 (The Procession with Palms)
Isaiah 50:4–7
Psalm 22
Philippians 2:6–11
Luke 22:14–23:56

. . . found human in appearance, he humbled himself. . . .

The conflict between good and evil, truth and lies, has been building. The untying of a colt signifies the final unleashing of forces that will collide in the experience we call the Passion. In Luke's account there are no palm branches waved and placed on the road, only cloaks—the outer garment that discloses so much about the one who wears it. And much is about to be disclosed. A "whole multitude of disciples" is present, mirroring the magnitude of betrayal that will occur. They are filled with praise, proclaiming, "Peace in heaven and glory in the highest." Indeed, this is an event of cosmic proportions, for Jesus tells the protesting Pharisees even if these disciples were to keep silent, the stones themselves would cry out.

As the events unfold, Jesus appears as one who knows and understands. With death imminent, he seems confident of the role he has agreed to play. During the final days of his life he has been doing what for him has always been essential. Every day he teaches in the temple, for "all the people would get up early each morning to listen to him" (Lk 21:38). At night he returns to the Mount of Olives, the place where he goes to pray.

The passage from Isaiah describes the one known as "the suffering servant," the one who gives his back to those who beat him, the one who does not shield his face from buffets and spitting. This servant is the one who remains faithful regardless of the cost, even when the price is death itself. But the confidence reflected in the composure he maintains comes from the relationship that has been his grounding all along: "The Lord God is my help, therefore I am not disgraced." In the face of mockery and abuse, there will be no shame.

In the passage from Philippians we are reminded that, while knowing who he is, while grounded firmly in the relationship with the Holy One, Jesus retains his humanity. Though come from God, he is fully human. He has chosen humanity and will not abandon humanity—his own and ours. What does it mean to be human? It means living in a tension between the propensity to choose self over others and the longing to connect to others in love. Being human means having the potential to be godlike, while struggling against the tug and pull of fear. The human Jesus experiences these tensions and does not falter, but continues in each and every moment to choose life. In this passage of scripture, he is the supreme model for us. He empties himself. He clears out egocentricity and self-absorption. And he listens—obedient—even in the presence of death.

The gospel readings make clear that something monumental is happening. Placed side by side are contrary elements that highlight the conflict. We are in a time and place that has no room for hedging, that leaves no possibility for equivocating. This is a battle between good and evil, and in this battle there can be no neutrality. The clashes are evident everywhere. The Eucharistic meal, symbol of the greatest act of fidelity, occurs in a setting rife with infidelity and betrayal. Gestures of friendship bump up against acts of denial and desertion. Humility and gracious service unfold in the midst of arguments about who is the greatest. The truth that is spoken can barely be heard over the fierce defense of illusion. Love is met by fear. Connectedness is met by the impulse to break away and run. The lines are clearly drawn. The only question that remains is, "Where do I stand?"

It is in Luke's gospel that Jesus cries out from the Cross, "forgive them, they know not what they do." Jesus does know. He sees before him the consequences of living in the illusion that we are separate and set apart, and he knows that fidelity comes from remaining connected to a faithful God. He knows that choosing life comes from remaining connected to the giver of life. And he knows that fear is no match for love, when love is given a chance.

The readings of this day urge us to look at our own lives. They call us to know what we do—and to be clear about the ramifications of all our actions. We have spent six weeks looking at our lives, examining the places where we have been superficial or slow. We have endeavored to rend our hearts and keep them open, exposed to God's gaze. We have tried to be honest, we have tried not to resist, we have tried to make a return to love. We have acknowledged the fear that tempts us to be lesser selves, and we have been in touch with our longing for "something new," something only the Holy One can give. Today's gospel ends with the image of a broken and lifeless body, taken down from a cross and laid in a borrowed tomb. For the time being, it looks as if evil and its cohort death have won. Of course we know that the story will continue, and we know how it will end for Jesus—with life. But today we are invited to reflect on how the story will end for each of us, for all of us. Life? Only if we choose it.

For Reflection/Journaling:

- Where do I stand?
- I bring my reflection to prayer. . . .

Holy Thursday

Scripture Readings:
  Exodus 12:1–8, 11–14
  Psalm 116
  1 Corinthians 11:23–26
  John 13:1–15

This is my body.

This is a day of remembrance and reversals, of strange juxtapositions that speak to realities not readily articulated. This is a moment in which particular events have universal significance and archetypal energies are expressed in utmost simplicity. The setting is that of Passover, old and new.

The passage from Exodus recalls the liberation of the Hebrews from slavery. The event revolves around a meal prepared in haste by people at the ready. The bread is unleavened and the herbs bitter. The lamb whose blood is used to mark the doorposts and lintels, signaling the Destroyer to pass over, is also the lamb who is consumed, eaten to provide food for the journey ahead, a reminder that liberation requires the risk of moving forward, not the comfort of staying put.

This is the meal that our Jewish brothers and sisters share each year to commemorate what God has done in their lives. Our own commemoration is a reminder that our journey is connected to theirs, or perhaps better said, that our journey is one with theirs—a journey of liberation of the human heart. We are indebted to the listening obedience that provides the foundation for our own relationship with God. And so today's reading from the Hebrew scriptures links us to both the past and the present as well as to those who are connected to us through a shared desire for the God whose name is Love.

It is clear that this ritual of remembrance is not only about the past. It is about us. It is about now. The reading from First Corinthians reminds us that the sharing of the bread and wine is to continue, keeping alive the hope that is ours. The bread that is broken and consumed recalls the body that is consumed by love and broken. The wine poured out represents blood not only spilled but transfused into those who believe, carrying life throughout the body. When we share this sacred meal we are proclaiming Jesus' death, announcing it as good news, because with death comes resurrection—his and ours.

Remembering what Jesus has done and continues to do is essential, but it is only part of what the meal signifies. We, too, are to become body and blood. We, too, are to be consumed by love and given over to death. The spirit of Jesus will be the leaven that allows us to rise. And then we will be broken. The love of Jesus will course through our veins so that we continue to live, so that life will be carried throughout the Body that is both his and ours. In this meal—in this communion—we become one, united with the one who brings salvation to all creation. In this meal we both remember what Jesus has done and commit ourselves to do the same.

The Jesus we see in the gospel passage is one who is attentive to the events unfolding around him. No doubt his own communion with the Holy One has brought him to this place. He is decisive, resolute, "fully aware." With death looming, Jesus focuses his attention on his beloved disciples and friends, and his intention is to leave with them a lesson they must never forget: he washes their feet. During supper—in the middle of the meal—he washes their feet. The task cannot be a pleasant one in a day and age when feet came into contact with rough surfaces and unsanitary matter. It was a disgusting task that a master could not demand of a servant, yet Jesus makes the washing of his disciples' feet a requirement for discipleship. When Simon Peter (both names are used, because this night he is both "Simon" and "Peter") resists, he is rebuked by Jesus who tells him, "Unless I wash you, you will have no inheritance with me." Unless you are willing to respond to others with gentle care, ready to receive as well as to give, committed to a leadership that is humble in its service, then you cannot be part of the dream. The dream is about connectedness in love, and anything less will open the door for fear. Jesus tells his disciples—and us—"I have given you a model to follow," and he leaves no room for equivocation.

On this night Jesus sets in motion two very significant rituals. One tells us *who* we are, the other tells us *how* we are to be. Viewed together, they convey much about who Jesus is—and who the Holy One is. Both the sharing of the Eucharistic meal and the washing of feet teach us to be receptive to the love that God longs to give. We must enter into the process with an openness and vulnerability that allows us to die to our egocentric wants and our fear-filled illusions. And then we must participate, becoming part of an organic process of transformation that continues not only to heal us but to heal all others as well. Participation in this mystery of love will begin the work that leads to the fulfillment of our deepest desire and the completion of God's beautiful dream.

For Reflection/Journaling:

- I imagine Jesus washing my feet. I imagine washing the feet of those I love most, of those I cannot love very well. I imagine each of them washing my feet.
- I hold a piece of bread and consider what it means.
- I bring my reflection to prayer. . . .

Good Friday

Scripture Readings:
   Isaiah 52:13–53:12
   Psalm 31
   Hebrews 4:14–16; 5:7–9
   John 18:1–19:42

Everyone who belongs to the truth listens to my voice.

It is easy to want to stand separate and apart today. It is tempting to want to divide the world into "us" and "them." But this, we know, is illusion. As much as we long not to be, we are connected to evil. The reading from Isaiah is graphic in its description of the human cruelty of which all of us are part. Normally without intention, we participate in sin-filled systems that are instruments of both justice and injustice, healing and pain. We are inextricably bound, intricately connected to the evil as well as to the goodness in the world. To fail to grasp this truth suggests that we have eyes but cannot see. We call this Friday "Good" because it *is* good for us to recognize that not all of our connections are pure, as much as we desire them to be.

But as difficult as this recognition of the nature of our connectedness is, as painful as it is for us to grasp how thoroughly *all* of life is connected, this is our good news as well. It is our connectedness to Jesus who lives in connectedness to the Holy One that is our salvation. The gift that Jesus gives is his refusal to become disconnected from Love. Neither fear nor death separates him from the Holy One. Even as he cries out, "My God, my God, why have you abandoned me?" he is tenaciously connected to the one he calls "Father." Even as he hangs on the Cross and utters the words "forgive them, for they know not what they do," he is thoroughly connected to humankind. From the Cross he stands in the breach, refusing to let go of God, refusing to let go of humanity. It is this refusal to allow the connection between the human and divine to be broken that saves us. Because of his love we can remain connected to the Holy One, and to the holy dream.

On this day we are reminded that the good news is not merely a good theory. The Passion of Jesus was real. The denial and the betrayal were real. The blows to his body and the nails driven into his flesh were real. The physical and emotional pain and suffering were real. Betrayed by a disciple and deserted by the ones he called friends, the fully human Jesus stood alone and remained faithful to Love. The intimacy of his relationship with the Holy One did not remove the anguish and agony of this moment, even as it allowed him to remain steadfast.

On this day as we once again allow the story to touch our hearts, we recognize that Jesus does not stand in the breach for himself. He is there on our behalf. But his standing in the breach does not exempt us from the same difficult task. He is the source of quantum grace for us, he shows us how the standing is done—but we, too, are to stand in breaches. We, too, are to be active participants in the ongoing passion and death that makes way for resurrection after resurrection. We, too, must suffer the cross, that point where love and fear meet—a place that is excruciating and terrifying and brings us to an agonizing confrontation with death. But it is the place where love is always victorious, even in those times we may not see it.

In the place where love and fear meet we can usually find a power struggle. As Pilate's fear increases, he says to Jesus, "Do you not know that I have power to release you and I have power to crucify you?" Pilate's power, distorted by fear, contributes to the atrocity at hand. It is power infused with fear that ruptures connections and creates breaches everywhere. Power in the hands of love—the way Jesus holds it—manifests as empowerment, calling others to discover their own power and use it cocreatively to choose life in a way that contributes to the healing and wholeness of all. What we commemorate this day is the process that is the source of our empowerment. Love met fear, and Love won, definitively, absolutely.

It is fitting that we leave our liturgical celebration in silence. There is much for us to ponder, much for us to absorb. The liturgy questions us. Will we allow ourselves to be moved? Will we allow what we have witnessed to be a good story, or will we allow it to become the good news it is intended to be? During the first week of Lent we heard the exhortation from Deuteronomy to "choose life." For six weeks we have been considering what is life-giving and what is not, what contributes to connectedness and what does not. Let us bring all that we have experienced—from the initial rending of our hearts to this moment of truth at the cross—into the silence, and then let us hear the words of Jesus as he says, "Everyone who belongs to the truth listens to my voice."

For Reflection/Journaling:

- Is there something that prevents me from standing in the breach between love and fear? What is it—and what do I want to have happen?

- I enter into silence and listen for the voice of truth.
- I bring my reflection to prayer. . . .

Easter Vigil

(Cycles A, B, C)

Scripture Readings:
Genesis 1:1–2:2
Genesis 22:1–18
Exodus 14:15–15:1
Isaiah 54:5–14
Isaiah 55:1–11
Baruch 3:9–15, 32–4:4
Ezekiel 36:16–17a, 18–28
Romans 6:3–11
Matthew 28:1–10 (A)
Mark 16:1–7 (B)
Luke 24:1–12 (C)

Do not be afraid.

This is a night for considering our connections. The liturgy is lengthy, filled with the scriptures and symbols that have fashioned us and continue to remind us who we are.

We begin in darkness filled with anticipation. Then comes the fire as we pray: "May the light of Christ, rising in glory, dispel the darkness of our hearts and minds." The Exsultet breaks forth with "Rejoice, heavenly powers! Sing, choirs of angels! Exult, all creation!" Then we enter into a night of storytelling that provides a panoramic view of the history of our journey with the Holy One.

We listen to the account of Creation and hear once again how the Holy One has a vision that includes us. Human beings are made in the image and likeness of God and are given dominion over all living things. We are called to be cocreators in a divine plan that is "very good."

We revisit the story of Abraham and Isaac and listen to the account of Abraham's test in which God asks him to sacrifice his only son, the son who is the symbol of God's promise to Abraham. As the story unfolds we see in Abraham a devotion to the divine that holds nothing back, no matter how heart-wrenching and absurd the surrender appears to be. Then, as we listen to the passage from Exodus, we envision God telling Moses to stretch out his staff, and watch as the sea miraculously parts in front of the Israelites who are fleeing from their captivity in Egypt and beginning the desert trek that will hone their character and shape their future as the people of God.

From Isaiah we hear gentle words of hope. To those who have strayed, the Holy One promises "with great tenderness I will take you back." The God whose love endures assures us "my love shall never leave you." And then we hear the invitation to "come." All who are thirsty, come. All who have no money, come. The invitation is persistent, and we begin to recognize that this night is not only about recalling what God has done, but about remembering who we are—the beloved of God.

The reading from Baruch instructs us to learn prudence, strength, and understanding and to know wisdom. These virtues will help us become who we are meant to be.

Through Ezekiel we remember the pain of infidelity and exile and the God who will not let us go but promises "you shall be my people, and I will be your God."

In the epistle to the Romans, Paul reminds these believers of their connection to the mystery commemorated this night. Baptism is the sign that we have said yes to participating in the death of Christ Jesus so that "we too might live in newness of life." Through participation in that death we "grow into union" with Christ, and in that union is our resurrection. If we die with Christ, we will also live with Christ, Paul says. This process, we have learned, is the heart of discipleship. Living the life we call "Christian" involves ongoing dying and rising, ongoing death to egocentricity and superficiality, ongoing transformation into love.

The climax of the storytelling comes with the reading of the gospel. After the sabbath, at daybreak, the women who have accompanied Jesus from Galilee return to his burial tomb with spices to anoint his body. In Matthew's account (Cycle A), there is a great earthquake. To be sure, this is an event so significant that Earth itself trembles. An angel "whose appearance was like lightning" tells the women not to be afraid and instructs them to announce to the men that Jesus has been raised, is on his way to Galilee, and will meet them there. When these disciples encounter the risen Christ they embrace his feet and hear the same words the women had heard earlier: "Do not be afraid."

In Mark's gospel (Cycle B) Mary Magdalene, Mary, the mother of James, and Salome bring spices to anoint Jesus' body. They are concerned about the very large stone that has been rolled against the door of the tomb. Who will roll it back? When they arrive at the tomb they are amazed, for the stone has already been rolled out of the way and a young man sitting in a white robe announces the good news that Jesus has been raised and is going before them to Galilee.

There are two men "in dazzling garments" in Luke's gospel (Cycle C), who appear to the puzzled women who wonder what to make of the empty tomb. "Why do you seek the living one among the dead?" these men ask. The women are terrified, but listen as the men remind them that events have unfolded just as Jesus said they would. He was handed over to sinners, crucified, then rose on the third day. Believing, they run back to tell the others who thought their story "seemed like nonsense." But Peter gets up, dashes to the tomb, and sees burial cloths lying in a heap.

The account of the Resurrection is *the* story of our faith. It is the experience of quantum grace for which the Israelites have been praying throughout the centuries. It is the fruition of the hopes of a people and the dreams of our God. It is an event that stands apart from all others, the great divide that separates this moment from every moment before and after. But we must not think that this is the end of the story, for it is only the beginning.

No matter which of the three gospel accounts is read, there is a common thread woven throughout: "Do not be afraid." We often note that the men around Jesus flee as the events of Good Friday unfold. But there is also a time when the women flee—and this is it, the moment they learn of the Resurrection. In Mark's gospel (in the verse after the liturgical reading concludes) we are told that the women "fled from the tomb, seized with trembling and bewilderment" (16:8).

The women were accustomed to being powerless, so accustomed that they were not tempted to run away from the awful reality of the Crucifixion. They could stay put on the fringe of the action, knowing that nothing would be asked of them, nothing would be challenged. They were essentially invisible, a danger to no one. But now, witnessing the Resurrection, they are terrified. Could their terror here imply that they intuitively grasp the meaning of the Resurrection all too well? Jesus, against cultural norms, has included women in his life and ministry. He has challenged social and religious convention, to be sure, but he has also challenged the women, just as he challenged the men, to be fully human. For those men who exercise various degrees of power, there is temptation to misuse or abuse power, to use it for ill gain and egocentric purposes. For women who have had no power, perhaps the temptation is to refuse to use power at all, to remain harmless inhabitants of the fringe.

The Resurrection, that place where love and fear have met, where fear has been defeated in and through Christ, gives us power. But we must claim that power and live empowered if the Resurrection is to have any effect. The Resurrection does not eliminate fear, it simply defeats it. Our task is to disengage from the fear so that we can choose life and live connected to one and all in love.

For Reflection/Journaling:

- I consider my own life. Where does fear interfere with resurrection? Are there places within me where I long to flee? I hear the words wash over me: "Do not be afraid."
- I bring my reflection to prayer. . . .

Easter Sunday

(Cycles A, B, C)

Scripture Readings:
  Acts 10:34a, 37–43
  Psalm 118
  Colossians 3:1–4 or 1 Corinthians 5:6b–8
  John 20:1–9

. . . a little yeast leavens all the dough . . .

While it is still dark, early in the morning, Mary of Magdala comes to the tomb in which her beloved Jesus has been laid. The day before had been the sabbath, the day of rest, but how restless Mary must have felt! How agonizing the in-between time must have been for her—that time between laying his body in the tomb and this moment when, finally, she can steal away to be with him again, even if there is no longer life in him. How horrified she must have been to arrive at the crack of dawn and discover that the tomb itself had been cracked open and the stone rolled away.

Her immediate thought is that someone has taken the body away, and without further exploration she runs to tell Simon Peter and the other disciples what has happened. Peter and "the other disciple" run to the tomb. The other disciple, running faster, stoops, looks into the tomb, and sees the burial cloths, but does not go in. When Simon Peter arrives, he enters the tomb and sees not only the burial cloths but the cloth that had covered Jesus' head rolled up in a separate place.

The scripture captures the moment for us, this moment of discovery that will alter the disciples' lives—and ours—forever. But Mary and Simon Peter and the others do not know this yet. They run. They hesitate. They see without knowing what it is they see. They only know that something significant, something outside their present ability to grasp, has occurred. It is not until the end of the account that the light begins to dawn, with that first disciple who sees and believes.

The narrative from the book of Acts stands in vivid contrast to that of the gospel. Peter—no longer called Simon—is speaking to those who have gathered in Caesarea. No longer running or hesitant, but standing firm, he tells his listeners that he and the other disciples have been witnesses to what God has done through the anointing of Jesus of Nazareth. He speaks openly of his association with Jesus, of his death and resurrection. He tells his listeners that the risen Jesus was visible to some of them, ate and drank with some of them, and then commissioned them to preach and testify to what they have seen and heard. Peter announces that everyone who believes will receive forgiveness of sins through Jesus' name.

The Epistle readings help us to understand what has happened between Mary's pre-dawn visit and Peter's confident preaching. "For you have died, and your life is hidden with Christ in God" (Col 3:3). The disciples have died to fear and have been caught up in the Love that defeats fear. Their lives are hidden with Christ, connected in Christ and connected to one another, and the connectedness continues to strengthen and encourage them. Having outgrown their timidity and uncertainty, they continue to grow and continue to announce the good news.

The passage from First Corinthians uses the image of yeast to describe the effect of the Resurrection upon believers. The "old yeast, the yeast of malice and wickedness," need no longer permeate our lives. We can clear out the old yeast and become a fresh batch of dough, celebrating a feast, not with the old but with "the unleavened bread of sincerity and truth."

The image of leaven is helpful and hopeful. Choosing life, choosing love, striving to live in genuine connectedness, can often make us feel quite alone. There will be days when we ask ourselves why we bother to be such idealists in a world that routinely values pragmatism over principles. When we speak the truth we have heard, there will always be others who ask, like Pilate, "What is truth?" and cast a skeptical eye in our direction. When we talk of healing breaches there will be those who tell us that there have always been breaches and there will always be breaches, so just keep your own state of affairs in order and you'll be fine. When we give voice to the conviction that we are all connected, that we are all one, that we are created to live in unity, our words will likely be drowned out by those who prefer to live under the illusion that we are separate and apart. And we will not be able to blame "them," for our own voices will join in at times, even when we don't want them to. These are the moments when we pray to be spared from the sin of superficiality.

During such times it will be good for us to remember the image of the yeast. Jesus is leaven for us, allowing hope to rise in the places of doubt and despair. Jesus calls us to be leaven, to be little pieces of truth and freedom, little particles of light and life, so that hope will continue to rise through-out the Body that is his, throughout the whole world.

Let us never doubt the necessity of grace as we strive to live the life that Jesus calls us to live. Like Peter, like Mary of Magdala, like all who have gone before us in faith, we are dependent upon the love and mercy of the Holy One. Like Peter and Mary and all the others, we will not be denied when we ask, for we have a God of love who longs for us to come, longs for us to open our hearts, longs to fill us to over-flowing with quantum grace. Then, and only then, we will experience our own resurrection, living in connectedness with all creation and the Holy One. Then, and only then, will God's dream be fulfilled.

For Reflection/Journaling:

- I examine a place in my life in which I have chosen res-urrection. I consider how my choosing has helped to cre-ate or repair my connectedness to self, others, God.
- I look for the places of resurrection in my life right now. I speak to the Holy One about the new life there, and ask for wisdom to cooperate with its unfolding.
- I bring my reflection to prayer. . . .

March 19: St. Joseph's Day

Scripture Readings:
2 Samuel 7:4–5a, 12–14a, 16
Psalm 89
Romans 4:13, 16–18, 22
Matthew 1:16, 18–21, 24

"When Joseph awoke, he did as the angel of the Lord had commanded him and took his wife into his home."

Much has been made of Joseph and his attentiveness to dreams. We admire him for his ability to hear God well and live in fidelity to what he heard, even when the message went against social convention. What a model parent he was for his infant son.

We know that Jesus was all about connectedness. He was connected to the Holy One in a depth of love we can only imagine. Sometimes we tend to forget that Jesus was fully human—and all that his full humanity implies. Fully human, he was filled with a longing for the holy. Fully human, he knew that his identity rests in connectedness. Fully human, he was bound to others in relationship, finding that in and through relationships he came to know more fully the Holy One.

We know that human beings have an innate longing for relationship, and we also know that this longing has to be honed by experience and tempered with wisdom. We long to relate by nature; we learn to relate by nurture.

This brings us back to Joseph. For faithful Jews in first-century Palestine, the father-son relationship was fundamental. It was the father who had primary responsibility for passing on life skills to the son. It was the father who taught the son his craft. It was the son who was at the father's side day after day, learning not only about occupation but dedication—how to live a life of fidelity to the living God.

Joseph was Jesus' primary teacher, and from what we know about Joseph and what we know about Jesus, we can perhaps fill in a few blanks in the story of their relationship. Joseph listened to the voice of God; Jesus listened to the voice of God. Joseph's listening—*ob audire*—was confirmed by his obedience; Jesus was obedient to the point of death. Jesus lived a life of connectedness, ever attentive to all the relationships in his life—including unconventional relationships with the marginalized, with women, with children, with the lepers and the lame, with the righteous and the profane.

Where did Jesus learn that relationships are primary? Isn't this the lesson for which his earthly father is most remembered? Joseph chose relationship over appearance when he kept Mary as his betrothed and took her into his home. He chose obedience to a God he could not see over cultural traditions that pressed in on every side. Surely this was the energy that surrounded the young Jesus as he grew in wisdom and stature at Joseph's side.

And so today we remember Joseph and honor him, for he taught Jesus the language of connectedness. He taught Jesus how to choose life through attentiveness to God's movements within his heart. He taught Jesus that relationships are more about one's connectedness with God than they are about one's contract with culture. He taught Jesus that love requires taking great risks, that freedom is more powerful than fear, and that death is no match for dreams.

For Reflection/Journaling:

- I recall a time in which the dream I carried seemed eclipsed by a bigger dream of God.
- I ask Jesus to tell me about Joseph.
- I imagine myself present in Joseph's carpenter shop and listen to the interaction between him and Jesus.
- I bring my reflection to prayer. . . .

March 25:
The Annunciation of the Lord

Scripture Readings:
  Isaiah 7:10–14; 8:10
  Psalm 40
  Hebrews 10:4–10
  Luke 1:26–38

May it be done to me according to your word.

During the season of Lent, when so many of the readings pull our attention back to "obedience" and "listening," it is fitting to look at Mary, the mother of Jesus. Throughout scripture the response of servants to God's call has always been some form of "Here I am. I come to do your will." So it is with Mary.

The Holy One sends the angel Gabriel to Galilee, to this young unmarried woman who lives in the village of Nazareth. We know nothing of Mary's life prior to the visitation, only what we can glean from the few details in the description of this extraordinary encounter. She is full of grace and has found favor with God. What kind of person is filled with grace? One who is open, who lives with a receptive heart, attentive to God's commandment to choose life and connect in love. To say that Mary is filled with grace implies that she has learned how to listen. Her response, we are told, is to "ponder" what sort of greeting Gabriel has given her, even as she is "greatly troubled" by what Gabriel says.

"Do not be afraid, Mary, for you have found favor with God," Gabriel responds. Divine favor comes as a surprise, an unexpected occasion of grace that startles Mary's imagination and catapults her into a place she never dreamed of going. God's favor rests on the one who is open and receptive to the gracious gift of a generous God. The announcement—a sign of the fulfillment of generation after generation of faithful Jewish people—is nevertheless unexpected when it comes. Gabriel tells Mary, "you will conceive in your womb and bear a son, and you shall name him Jesus."

Mary's response to Gabriel contains no resistance, only the question of how God's will might be accomplished. Although she cannot know the full significance of the visit and her yes, such a pondering, obedient woman must know that something truly difficult is being asked of her. Still, she does not resist, but simply continues to listen. God's favor does not come without support. God frequently provides companions when we are most in need. Often through the gift of relationships God confirms our hearing and encourages our call. In the account of the Transfiguration, that crisis moment in Jesus' life, God allows him to converse with Moses and Elijah. Their experience and wisdom must have supported Jesus as he continued to say yes. God now offers such support to Mary, as Gabriel reveals that her kinswoman Elizabeth is with child—another unexpected surprise for one who is grace-filled and who has found favor with God.

Meister Eckhart once said that we are all meant to be mothers of God, for Christ is always needing to be born. Our purpose as disciples is to continue to manifest the Incarnation, to continue to announce and enflesh "God with us." Mary becomes, then, an appropriate companion for us. Like Mary, we can become obedient listeners, open to hearing the messages and messengers of God. We can be filled with grace, making room in our hearts for the Word to visit. We can "find favor"—surprised by the Spirit who seeks out the open-hearted. We, too, can become impregnated by the Spirit, in countless ways giving birth to new life in our midst. Each of us, in our unique way, can be hailed as "full of grace," a cocreative partner in God's dream for humankind.

For Reflection/Journaling:

- Mary is afraid—"deeply troubled"—yet continues to say yes to the Spirit. I recall a time that I have done the same.
- I consider what keeps me from listening to God's invitations to me. Is there anything I want to ask God to heal?
- I visit with Mary and Elizabeth, listening to their thoughts and feelings.
- I bring my reflection to prayer. . . .

Judy Cannato is spiritual director at River's Edge: A Place for Reflection and Action at St. Joseph Center in Cleveland, Ohio and the author of *Quantum Grace: Lenten Reflections on Creation and Connectedness* (the daily readings). A retreat director and Certified Mid-Life Directions Consultant, she has master's degrees in education and religious studies from John Carroll University in Cleveland, and is the author of numerous articles on spirituality.

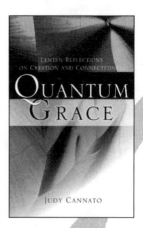